AYSCOUGHFEE

A GREAT PLACE IN SPALDING

With my best wishes

Nancy Snowdon

NANCY SNOWDON

Published by Nancy Snowdon
34 London Road Spalding PE11 2TE

ISBN 978-0-9557292-0-1

Design and Typeset by Patrick Wensor
Printed in the UK by Clearpoint Colourprint Limited

AYSCOUGHFEE

A GREAT PLACE IN SPALDING

NANCY SNOWDON

1909 postcard showing the Lake and Owl Tower

The same view showing the War Memorial in 2007

ACKNOWLEDGEMENTS

There are so many people I want to thank.

First and foremost to Patrick Wensor for his interest, knowledge, and enormous skill with all of his electronic gadgets in compiling the book and it's pictures. Most of the photographic work is his, and I have made use of his extensive collection of historical postcards.

Secondly to all of the subscribers, who have made this publication possible, and whose names have been listed at the end of the book.

The staff at the Sue Ryder bookshop in Spalding, which is the hub of local history interest and to Paul Radford in particular. I am also grateful to the editor and staff of the Lincolnshire Free Press & Spalding Guardian, for their help and for permission to include the old press cuttings from 1959 and 1898.

Thanks to English Heritage for permission to publish Mr. Prosser's report on Holyrood House for the first time.

Thanks to Dr. Jonathan Clark of Field Archaeology Specialists Ltd, for permission to use the diagrams from the 2005 Historic Building Assessment report on Ayscoughfee Hall.

The Nattes drawings are published courtesy of Lincolnshire County Council, from their Local Studies collection.

Images of the Pinchbeck Fen Map is used with permission from the National Archives at Kew

Acknowledgements go to Spalding Gentlemen's Society for the use of original images from the Museum.

Finally, my grateful thanks go to South Holland District Council for their offers of support and help in the production of this book.

I have made every effort to trace the copyright holders of all of the other pictures published, and I apologise in advance for any unintentional omissions. I will be pleased to insert any appropriate acknowledgements in any subsequent editions. The carved figures and grotesques at the end of some chapters are from the exterior of Ayscoughfee.

Nancy Snowdon
Summer 2007

Painting by Beatrice Parsons – from "The Charm of Gardens" published in 1910

FOREWORD

Our view of Spalding is often framed by the many Georgian and later buildings that Spalding still possesses. It is often forgotten that Spalding was a medieval town of some significance and wealth with many fine buildings in this period, including Ayscoughfee Hall, one of the main survivors. Immediately next door to Ayscoughfee was a further impressive building, known as Gayton Hall, sadly only demolished within the past fifty years. Our forbears often found it expedient to 'modernize' a medieval building by simply up-dating the front facade, while retaining the main original structure behind. This has often masked the true nature and age of a building from the casual viewer. As is explained by Nancy Snowdon in this volume, Ayscoughfee has received more than one face-lift which has altered its external appearance. There might even be further medieval buildings to be discovered in Spalding, currently unrecognized because of the changes that they have received over time.

The recently completed restoration and refurbishment of Ayscoughfee Hall had the additional dividend of facilitating an archaeological investigation into the building's fabric. This was the first time that Ayscoughfee had been subject to a systematic effort to understand its constructional history and historic layout. The archaeological work finally resolved much the speculation over the date, construction, and original planned form of the Hall. We now know that the building was erected according to a considered plan in one building campaign and must have been nearly complete in 1451 when the trees, which were to be used as the roof timbers, were being felled. It can now be acknowledged and appreciated as one of the most complete examples of a 15th century grand house built by the medieval mercantile class.

Although much was discovered by the archaeology of the building, our knowledge of the original builder and subsequent owners of Ayscoughfee remained unclear. Some documentary research had been undertaken, which high-lighted the existence of a series of inventories starting in the seventeenth century. Inventories were made to assess the value of the deceased owners goods and often list items on a room by room basis, providing significant information on the layout and use of rooms in a house at a given time. Perhaps most interesting of all is the existence of a will made by Nicholas Alwyn, son of the builder of Ayscoughfee, Richard Alwyn. In this will Nicholas describes Ayscoughfee as 'My great place of Spalding', a description which is still accurate. But who were the Alwyns and why did they build such a fine house in Spalding?

Within this volume Nancy Snowdon has sought to answer these questions and other enigmas by drawing together more detailed information on the individuals who were part of the Ayscoughfee story, exploring their backgrounds, motivations and deeds. As Nancy shows, the Ayscoughfee story is at the centre of the history of Spalding, and what a fascinating story it is.

Dr Jonathan Clark
York, 2007

WHY THIS BOOK HAD TO BE WRITTEN

Spalding may seem an unexpected place to discover an unknown national treasure but in 2005 historians' research revealed just how unique is Ayscoughfee Hall, with its inexplicable and unpronounceable name.

The house sits in the central part of busy Spalding town, surrounded by teeming traffic, parking congestion and overcrowded narrow streets. Suddenly, there is the ancient Hall facing the river in its own extensive and peaceful gardens with gravelled walks, yews, green lawns and flower beds, a timeless haven. Ayscoughfee Hall has been, for so long, part of the town's life.

And all because six hundred years ago a wealthy London merchant decided to build himself a grand mansion in his family's home town, Spalding. His creation has remained virtually unchanged ever since and has never, until now, been acknowledged as a unique piece of domestic architecture; nor has it borne its founder's name for posterity to remember him by. Concealed by Victorian Gothic frills and furbelows on the outside of the house, much of the structure has remained intact. In his will, Sir Nicholas Ailwyn called it 'My Great Place'.

Spalding has no public park or recreation ground and this must be one of the main reasons why Ayscoughfee Hall and gardens have played an especially important part in the life of Spalding people. Acquired by the citizens of Spalding between 1898 and 1902 "for their recreation", the gardens have been enjoyed and remembered by generations of children. The walks, gardens, bowls and tennis courts are cherished. Pride has been taken in the unique setting of the local Tourist Information Office (now gone), the famous bird collection (now lost to Leicester Museum) and the bandstand (now burnt down). All are lamented by the old Spaldonians. Although its importance has never been fully appreciated, and certainly never recognised as a national treasure, it has been fully used and the source of great local pride. So great was the local interest an introductory session for the restoration project in 2005 had to be repeated three times to overflowing audiences in the large hall of South Holland Centre.

This proprietorial enthusiasm for a local building and garden so little known outside the town has been fuelled by the recent discovery that it is almost unique, a most important medieval building. This news startled Spalding out of its complacency.

So little is known about Ayscoughfee, so much taken for granted; there is virtually no literature readily available. Strangely, no one yet has even undertaken a full research programme as to the beginnings of Ayscoughfee. Plenty of traditional mild interest and wild conjectures but no one has succeeded in establishing how it came to be built or the real reason for its peculiar name. No ancient records appear to have survived.

Many local historians, old Robin Harmstone (1846), Alderman Gooch (1940) and others told their traditional tales which have been repeated in the absence of any reliable information. David Roberts,[1] writing in 1975, points out many interesting features, referring to the 'little known' Ayscoughfee Hall, claiming that it was well worth further investigation. He was the first to draw attention to the face behind the veil.

Rosalyn Pursglove produced a workman-like booklet in 1994 whilst she was working in the South Holland Museum Service. Spalding Free Press Publications and South Holland District Council have produced various pamphlets and information sheets. Recently,[2] Dr. Jonathan Clark wrote about the refurbishment of 'Ancient Ayscoughfee'. The strange name 'Ayscoughfee' has never been explained. Although the famous Lincolnshire family called Ayscough has never been known as a Spalding family, many assumptions have been made for the unusual name. What is there to link the house with the Ayscough family? What is meant by the Fee of Ayscough? And why have its founders and builders, father and son, Richard and Nicholas Ailwyn, been so long neglected?

---

1. Lincolnshire History and Archaeology 10. 36-47
2. 'Lincolnshire Unearthed'. Issue 4. Autumn 2005

Postcard sent from the author's present house in Spalding, dated 28th April 1915

To Miss Eliza Smythe,
Millard Place,
Liphook,
Hants

"Enjoying myself here, and having fine dry weather, though cold. Hope you are well and able to get out a little. A lot of poor Belgian Refugees here; have spoken to some. All news when I see you."

C.M.Russell

AYSCOUGHFEE TIMELINE

1451	Oaks felled for the roof timbers.
1450-52	House built for the Ailwyn Family.
1499	Richard Ailwyn's son Sir Nicholas Ailwyn, a member of the Mercer's Company, becomes Lord Mayor of London.
1505/6	Nicholas Ailwyn leaves his lands and tenements in Southwark and Spalding to his son Francis and then his grandson Nicholas.
1520-56	Unknown occupiers, perhaps the Gayton or Hall families ?
1556	Reginald Hall inherits the property on the death of his mother.
1602	Thomas Wimberley buys the house from Robert Hall.
1616	Thomas Wimberley dies leaving the property to his son Beville Wimberley.
1641	Beville Wimberley dies passing the house to his sister Elizabeth Evington, who was later married to Dymoke Walpole after the death of Nicholas Evington.
1658	Dymoke Walpole's eldest son Sir John Walpole, sells the house to John Johnson of Pinchbeck for £400.
c.1720	Yew walks planted, creating vistas within the gardens - tree-ring dating in the 1990s has confirmed that one of the yews dated from this period.
1732	Formal gardens are shown on the map by John Grundy.
c.1770	The "Owl Tower", a square building consisting of a room built on four pillars, was built at the end of the lake.
1794	The yews in front of the Hall are felled.
to	Adam style ceiling installed in Great Hall, and gallery built.
1830	New main and back staircases installed.
	Kitchen built adjacent to north wing (shown in 1818 Burgess painting).
	Wooden framed Gothic windows installed at the front of the house.
1819	The original avenue of chestnut trees planted between Ayscoughfee Hall and Holyrood House.
1845	The front windows are replaced in stone, with bays added in the cross-wings. The current porch and colonnade is installed.
	The turret on the tower is raised, and the north service wing added.
1851	The last of the Johnsons leaves the Hall, having been resident there for two centuries.
1852-96	The partially furnished Hall is rented out.
1898	The Hall & Gardens are sold by Isabella Johnson to a Committee of Spalding citizens for £2100 The property is bought as a gift to the town in commemoration of Queen Victoria's Diamond Jubilee.

1902 The property is handed over to the town free of debt on August 9th in celebration of the Coronation of King Edward VII. The Hall is then held in trust by the Spalding Urban District Council for the people of Spalding.

1908 The first bowling green laid out.

1915-20 Hall is used by the War Office to house Belgian Refugees.

1920 The first tennis courts are installed where the current Aviary is.
One of the rooms is rented out to a Miss Henry, who begins a Kindergarten Class. Later this successfully expands becoming Ayscoughfee Hall School (now based at Welland Hall in London Road).

1921 Despite a public outcry, the Owl Tower is demolished to make way for a new War Memorial for the town of Spalding.

1922 The War Memorial, built to a design by Sir Edwin Lutyens, is unveiled to the pubic.

1925 New tennis courts are laid out on their current site.

1931 June – an earthquake damages stonework at the front of the Hall, and breaks the glass of some of the windows.
September - a new coat of arms, carved out of a two-tonne block of Bath stone by Messrs Chapman & and Burns installed at the front of the Hall.
October - New ornamental gates were officially unveiled, dedicated to the memory of William Royce MP.

1937 A public lending library is created in the former Dining Room (currently The Geest Gallery).
A rustic Band Stand is built as part of the celebrations for the Coronation of George VI, and a fountain constructed in the lake.

1939-45 Land Girls occupy the Hall during the War, and Mr Tero, the Parks Superintendent, creates a model allotment on one of the tennis courts. Some birds in the aviary are killed and some buildings are damaged when a jettisoned bomb is dropped into the gardens.

1953 The 'British Birds' portion of the Ashley Maples Bird Collection (belonging to the Spalding Gentlemen's Society) is housed in the Hall after it's previous site in Red Lion Street runs out of space.

1957 The original chestnut trees from 1819 are felled.

1959 A gathering of 100 people witnesses the planting of eight young chestnut trees in the Avenue.

1966 Part of the Stable block is burned down.
The Public Lending Library moves out of the Hall and into Victoria Street.

1974 The Hall is now run by the South Holland District Council, which replaces the former Spalding Urban District Council.

1982 Ayscoughfee Hall School moves out of the house into the former Parish Church Day School buildings in Church Street.

1983-4 The Hall is rejuvenated with new Drainage Gallery and Geest Gallery.
Ayscoughfee Hall is made a Registered Charity.

1986 Museum officially re-opened, incorporating the Tourist Information Centre.

1996 Friends of Ayscoughfee is formed with the aim to build a new bandstand.

2003 Heritage Lottery Fund grants a total of £743,000 to SHDC, to "develop and improve all aspects of the museum…"
Hall closed for refurbishment under the supervision of Anderson & Glenn, Project Managers and Conservation Architects.

2006 The Hall is re-opened on 30th June by Dr Jonathan Clark.

CONTENTS

CHAPTER 1

ON THE BRINK OF THE WELLAND (THE TRIANGLE)

Spalding is an ancient place, perhaps settled in pre-Roman times. It may have been a port. The Romans[1] are said to have attempted to drain the boggy inland area by cutting the Westlode River, for the waters to drain into the Welland at Spalding as it flowed out into the sea. As Roman levels are now 15-20ft. under the town, nothing of note has been recorded about the Roman town.

Spalding in the fifteenth century was a small market town, clustered round the Priory, its nucleus, which stood near High Bridge in its large walled grounds. Nothing now delineates the site, which spread along the area behind the shops in Sheep Market, now private car parks. When it was demolished after the dissolution in 1540 the stones were dispersed to all sorts of buildings. The Priory itself virtually disappeared in the 16th century, with only the row of the Abbey Buildings remaining. Abbey Yard has disappeared. Vine Street is a memory of the Priory's vineyard. The main entrance stood at the side of the present sheep market at the end of what was called the Gore. The town revolved round the Priory, the leading and most powerful monastery in the Fens. The Prior had his own wharf for his fish delivery, his own fleet, his own estates and manors, a windmill and water mill for the monastery water supply and drainage.

Dugdale's sketch map (below) shows the town, St. Thomas' Road (**L**: *Strata S.Thomae*) and the site between the Westlode (**K**: *Aqua vocata Westload*) and the Welland (**G**: *Welland flumen*).

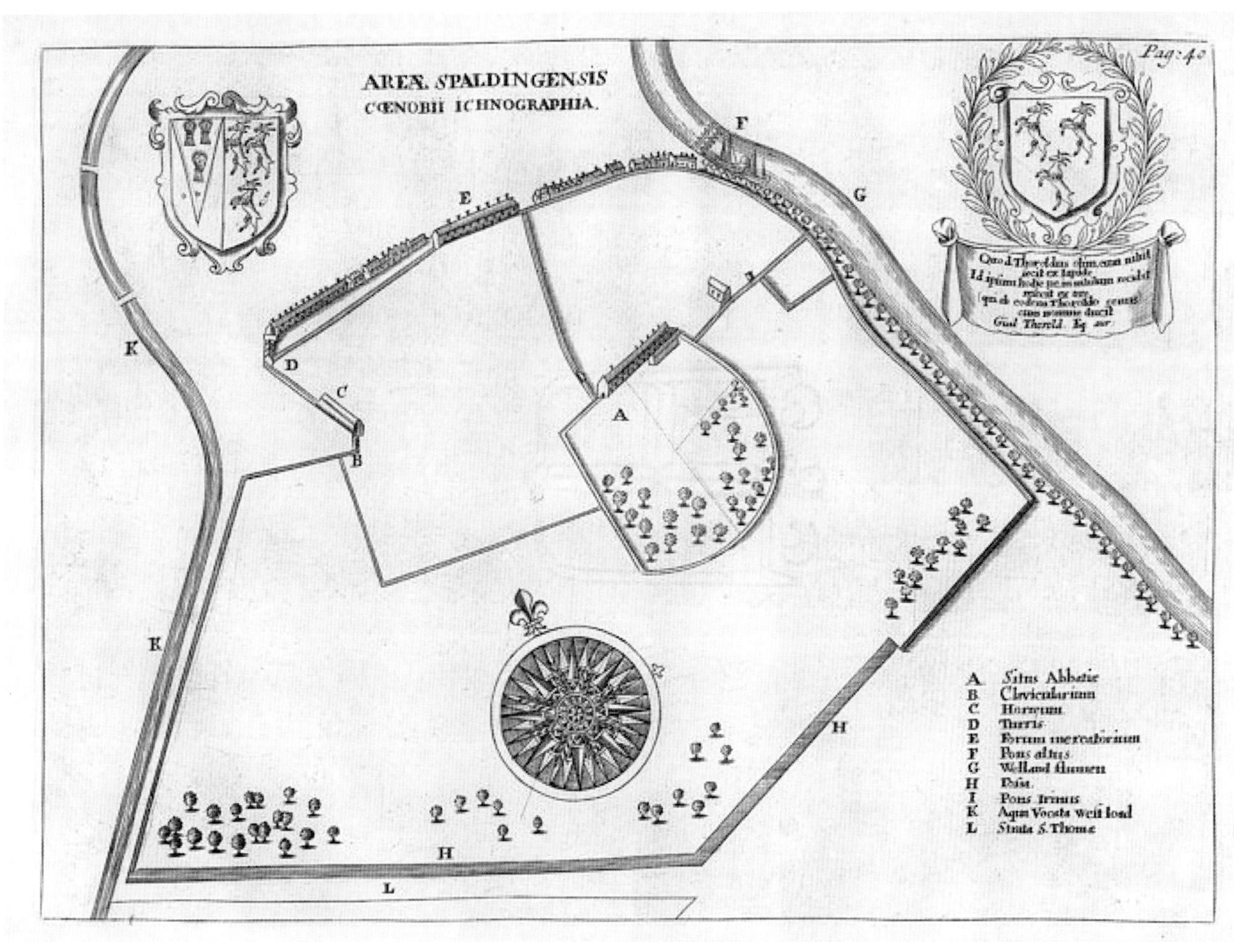

Sir William Dugdale's plan of Spalding, first published in 1655,
reprinted here from the 1718 edition of his *Monasticon Anglicanum*

The monastery was intended to be self sufficient, but the townspeople who settled had their own Parish Churches. Along the river[1] spread some houses, along with shipyards, warehouses and loading quays.

The two sides of the river, were joined by the original High Bridge known as *Pons Altus* (and said to be Roman). On the west brink were the town and the Benedictine Priory, while the east brink housed the Parish Church and the two great houses, Ayscoughfee Hall and Gayton House.

The riverside site on the east bank of the Welland as it runs through the old port of Spalding must, from the beginning of the settlement of the town, have been an important site. Just beyond the reaches of high tide it would have formed a safe mooring haven for shipping and was easily accessible to dry land by the river's low, sloping banks for loading and unloading boats.

Three ancient buildings, the new Parish Church and two grand houses, Gayton House (Holyrood, as it was called afterwards) and Ayscoughfee Hall, are collected together there on the east brink forming a triangle. Apart from the Priory Buildings on the other side of the River Welland, which are now completely obliterated (including the conventual chapel) these buildings were the oldest in the town.

South-east view of the Parish Church in 1823 by Hilkiah Burgess (SGS collection)

1. Although Bourne was the main Roman centre, there is much academic discussion about the extent of the water levels of the Welland, and the flooding of the Spalding area, whether early habitation was then possible so near the coast before the 5th century. *The Origins of a Fenland Community*. Neil Sumner 1987. Unpublished thesis.

The Parish Church was built on the brink of the Welland in 1284, the first of the three buildings and well documented. The Prior[1] built the new Parish Church of St. Mary and St. Nicholas[2] to replace two small churches which had been formerly used by the parishioners. These were on the other side of the river, one next to the conventual church within the Priory walls (St. Mary Stokys) and the other known as Holycross, *(Ecclesia S.Crucis)*, by the Market Stead.

The expanding population meant the churches were not big enough, particularly the graveyards. William of Littleport, the Prior known for his building projects, decided to use materials from the old churches and to build a new, larger church[3] on the other side of the Welland. The regular inundation of the area was also put forward as a reason, the new east brink site was less likely to flood.

An old cemetery chapel was already on that site, the chapel of the Blessed Thomas the Martyr and part of the old walls were incorporated into the new building. Nicholas Pevsner points out some of the early remains still identifiable.

The new church was completed by John's successor, Clement of Hatfield in 1318. Just as it was being completed a man called Richard-le-Skinner came forward with a most generous gift. The 14th century Richard Skinner, a local man trading in wools and hides, was a Merchant of the Staple and very prosperous; a leading merchant with continental contacts. He may have had tanning yards in Spalding. Barkers Row near the junction of the Welland and Westlode may have been the site. He wanted to build a special chapel to St. Thomas á Beckett and provided the necessary money and the chapel was built onto the general building with its own door at the side. A first floor was put in and for many years the top floor of the chapel was used as a school. If Nicholas Ailwyn went to school it would have been to this small establishment next to his home. It is remembered as a "little barn-like structure" with a stone staircase in the outside wall with a sort of concrete floor.[4] The door is still there but now closed up. Sometimes there was only one pupil attending but the school survived until it became the Spalding Grammar School. The Grammar School remained there until 1881.

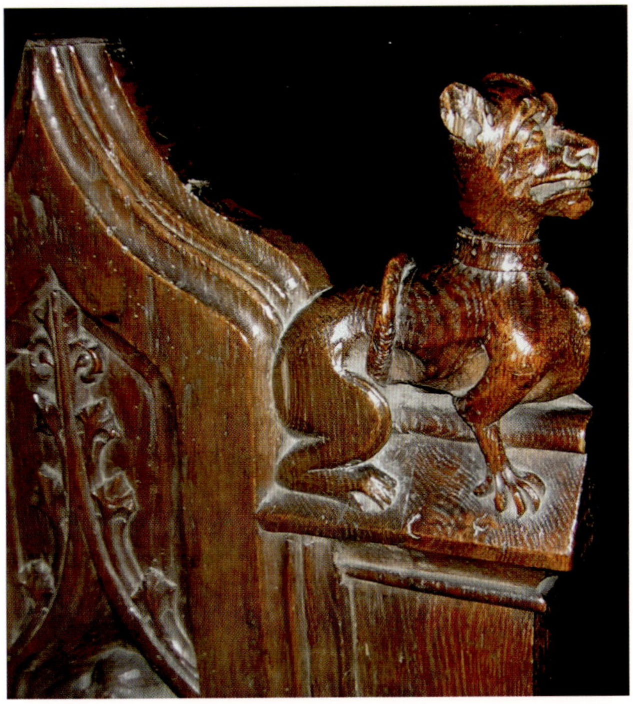

This chapel houses a medieval pew which is well concealed at the back almost out of sight. It has clearly been moved around the church. Parts of it are modern, and only the ends are medieval. The end of this pew has a large cat-like lion complete with smile, long tail, claws, a studded collar and the round ears of a bear.

1. The Spalding Prior had recently acquired the quarries at Barnack, a useful building stone, which was used for the church.
2. Probably first known as St. Mary; St. Nicholas being adopted later. There is some doubt about the number and names of all the various churches and chapels of the Priory and their exact situation.
3. N. Pevsner and John Harris *Lincolnshire 1964* p646. J. P. Hoskins, *The Story of the Parish Church of St. Mary and St. Nicholas* 1950. p15. *The East Wall.*
4. Described by Dr. Perry who was a pupil there in the 19th century.

Under the lion, which is crouching, a small 18" high figure is carved (left). A youth with bushy hair, a small felt hat, odd sleeves, a badge on his shoulder, clutching with both hands what looks like a harp.

The other end of the pew is still covered over by another piece of old wood.

This end panel (right) has a poppy head of fruit or flowers and may have originally been much bigger and is badly worn. Below it is a coat of arms, shield-shaped with a clear depiction of three animals.[1] They have been known as "the three bears"; but they have long tails, round ears and hooves. They look like sheep or lambs.

The coat of arms of the Ailwyns is reputedly "*three sable lions rampant argent on fesse engrailed azure*" or "*argent on fesse engrailed azure three lions rampant*". A "fesse engrailed" divides the animals. There is no doubt that this carving represents the Ailwyn coat, although there are variations, and this confirms his gifts to the church.

The history of this chapel is described by William Maratt:[2]

"Richard le Skinner of Spalding, a Merchant of the Staple, founded the chapel of B V [Blessed Virgin] and the Guild of St. Thomas the Martyr, consecrated by Walter, Lord Archbishop of Armagh; which being a Chantry is served by massing priests".

In 1315, the Prior of Spalding was Clement Hatfield, who entertained Edward II that year and died in 1317. The Bishop of Lincoln[3] was John de Dalderby (1300-1320). There seems no reason why an Irish Archbishop should be brought in to consecrate the new chapel; perhaps the Prior was too busy entertaining the young King Edward.

1. *Historical Spalding* Graham Smith. 1966
2. Bishop Dalderby in 1313, seemed to have been concerned with the lepers of St. Nicholas at Spalding, but is not mentioned otherwise in relation to the consecration. (Maratt p274).
3. W. Marratt. *The History of Lincolnshire(Topographical, historical and descriptive)* 1814.

There was formerly a carved rood screen which divided the chancel from the nave. This old rood screen is no longer in the church. It was removed before William Maratt wrote about it in 1814. It is not necessary to detail its journeyings but it is now standing outside, locked securely in the south porch, and in a very dilapidated state, exposed to some of the elements.

The screen is 15th century and ornately carved with foliage. The top border and cornice has three devices. The first is the wool sack, (shown on the right of this picture) which represents Spalding's wool production and also the Merchants of the Staple. To the right of the woolsack is the second device, the faded outline of the Maidenhead.

The third device may be the garbs[1] of the Earl of Chester's arms (adapted as part of the coat of arms of the Priory), or more likely may be hanging skins, the emblem of the Skinners.

The screen is difficult to photograph clearly, and the details are better seen first hand.

The most noteworthy device on the screen is the woman's head, which is the Mercers' Maiden, or Maidenhead, a deeply significant emblem of the Mercers Company, but definitely NOT the Virgin Mary. The Maiden is shown clearly on the remains of the cornice on the screen, and is wearing a pectoral cross.

The Mercers' arms are: "*Gules a demi virgin coped below the shoulders issuing from clouds all proper, vested or crowned with an Eastern crown of the last, her hair dishevelled, wreathed round the temples with roses of the second all within an orle of clouds proper*".

1. A garb is a sheaf of corn.

The identity of Richard le Skinner[1] remains mysterious. He must have been a man of some substance for this was a generous gift. He could have been a member of a very ancient family of Skynner or Skinner, from Bolingbroke and Thornton Curtis, whose arms were granted in 1557; originally their family came from Exeter and had no apparent connections outside North Lincolnshire, except they may have been connected with the Skinners of Boston[2] through the Skinners of Thornton Curtis, whose "ancient arms of his ancestors" were "*a lion rampant sable with an orle of eight crescents gules.*" The pedigree only starts in the 16th century, so the earlier Richard le Skinner may or may not be part of this family. Many members of the Skinner family were Mercers and were called Richard, and one was a Customs official in Boston in 1540. There is evidence they may have been connected with the wool trade. Richard le Skinner was a Merchant of the Staple (and his emblem was a black lion) which means he was probably not actually involved in skinning hides, in tanning, but this cannot be confirmed by the Skinners Livery Company, whose records of membership do not go back to the 14th century.

All sorts of interesting questions arise from this heraldry in the Parish Church. The lion on the pew end *may* be the lion of Richard the Skinner, the founder, although of course it is black now but it is recognisable as a lion but not correct in every respect. Who in Spalding would have seen a real lion? Early records show that Henry III had lions[3] in the Tower of London in 1262, but before that in 1235 there were leopards at the King's Park in Woodstock. There is reference to one leopard in the Tower (perhaps the others died) and a command for the "sustenance of the leopard" and his keeper. By 1343 there was one lion, one lioness, one leopard and two "cattes lions" in the Tower. There seems to have been some confusion about the difference between lions and leopards, but the pew end lion is recognisable, although the lamb-lions are a little doubtful, even for someone who had never seen a lion.

Starting with the Parish Church, where the carvings can actually be inspected, the first of the three ancient buildings gives several clues to the Skinner gift of the chapel[4] and of the later Ailwyns, who were benefactors, who lived at Ayscoughfee. There are no clues hidden at Gayton House because it no longer exists and that leaves Ayscoughfee Hall itself to scour for hints about its builders, the Ailwyn family. The Parish Church is full of clues which can now be interpreted. The medieval screen, now in the south porch, yields information and may well have been donated by Richard Ailwyn. In Nicholas' will, it is specifically mentioned. He required the screen to be gilded. It is also recorded that Richard Ailwyn presented a sanctus bell, which has long disappeared. But the interesting point is that the screen may not be the one referred to in the Will; it has no appearance of ever having been gilded as Nicholas wanted. A rood screen in a church would normally have one door in the centre; the object of it was to divide the chancel from the nave. This screen has signs of more than one doorway in its composition,[5] which could mean it was a domestic screen dividing off the kitchens. It has clearly been altered, perhaps removed from somewhere else and it might be possible that it was a domestic screen taken from Ayscoughfee Hall itself

1. *Miscellanea Geneologica et Heraldica*. Howard 1874. vol.I p80. *Arms of Skinner of Bolingbroke, Ermyns three lozenges sables on every one a fluore flowrdelices. Gold.*
2. *Skinner of Boston*. Maddison. Sir Vincent Skinner was a notorious mercer who built a house using the materials of Thornton Abbey, which collapsed, bankrupted him and he died in a debtors prison.
3. John Stone. *A Survey of London.* Oxford 1908
4. There is actual reference to William the son of Richard the Skinner in 1321, and a John Skinner endowed a Chantry in Cowbit in 1547.
5. Dr. Jonathan Clark, Director of Historic Buildings, has pointed this out.

Tracing its history has been tortuous. It was originally in place and described as 'perpendicular', then incorporated into a new screen, leaving ends embedded into the walls. It was then apparently cut up and used in various places, first in a screen between the clergy and servers' vestries. There is an older reference to a 'projection' in the centre, for which no explanation can be found, and it did not appear the screen had been recently inspected at the time of Francis Bond's book.[1] The octagonal staircase to the rood loft is still intact and continues to the roof of the nave. The original screen was part of the renovation of Sir Gilbert Scott[2] in 1870. When the church was again reorganised the medieval pieces were discarded and finished up in the south porch where they are seriously deteriorating.

The screen is the only piece of evidence confirming the Ailwyns' gift to the church, besides the carved pew ends and both might be preserved much more carefully, even though the screen is now in pieces.

The current rood screen, after restoration in 2007

1. *Screens and Galleries*. Francis Bond. 1908. p119.
2. *The Story of the Parish Church of St. Mary and St. Nicholas, Spalding*. J.P. Hoskins. (Revised 1950).

CHAPTER 2

GAYTON HOUSE

The second of the three buildings which formed part of the triangle was known as Gayton House. Nothing is left of it now. It stood there for 600 years, a neighbour to Ayscoughfee. Its name changed over the years, and in modern times it was called Holyrood[1].

Alderman Gooch claims that Gayton House was inhabited by the Gayton family 'who lived there in 1480'. He gives no source for this information. He did not claim they built it, but there is no doubt they existed and lived in Spalding.

After a long career, it had a miserable end. Purchased by a cinema company, it was then acquired by the local authority (then Spalding Urban District Council) to build a new town hall. Gayton was divided into flats for homeless people, and in 1959 it was brutally demolished.[2] Very little has been known about it; it was just as historically interesting and unusual as its neighbour, Ayscoughfee. On the site of Gayton now stands a brick-built modern office block; the road by its side is laughingly called 'The Vista'. Plans are now afoot to pull down the ugly modern pub on the other side of the Vista and replace it with a large mock-Georgian block of flats, taking up the riverside plot that was orchards and gardens of Gayton House, and a most attractive prospect.

The original Gayton House was an interesting building; side by side with Ayscoughfee. If it was there before the building of next door Ayscoughfee we shall probably never establish. But it formed a most attractive contrast to Ayscoughfee with its brick and timbered walls, a plain, long comfortable looking single storey building, perhaps with a thatched roof. Behind Gayton House, nearer the churchyard[3] or even partly in the churchyard, stood another building. When it fell into ruin is not known, but the stones[4] were still about and available in the 16th century for re-use. Tradition claims that this building was a Guild Hall or house for one of the several religious Guilds[5] of Spalding. St. John's and Holy Trinity had altars and small chapels in the Parish Church and there was also one to St. Mary. But St. Mary's Guild, dating from 1320, alone had a Guild house "*ex part orient ripe*" on the east brink[6] of the Welland. It has been referred to as the Masters or Wardens House of the Guild of St. Thomas, but is more likely to have been St Mary's. It is quite possible that Gayton House itself was the Guild, but more enquiries are needed.

There were various alterations[7] in the 16th century. It is said that the old stones from the 'Guildhall', then in ruins, were used to build 'offices', perhaps servants' quarters at the north end of Gayton House. About two hundred years later a southern extension with a staircase at the south was built. This has been explained by some for the name the 'Guildhall', because of the use of the old stones, but it may turn out that it was, in fact, the Guildhall building, and the 'ruins' were the service block at the rear – demolished earlier.

---

1. There was an ancient chapel somewhere on this site, called Holyrood, not to be confused with the church in the market place, demolished 1284.
2. It was referred to in July 1958 as a 'pile of rubble' and it was still in that condition in June 1959, so by the time the report by Mr. Prosser was written it was too late.
3. The 1779 Armstrong map of Spalding shows extensive buildings behind Gayton House, while the Grundy map (1730) shows none.
4. T. W. Townsend (1959) claims that when it was altered in the 16th century stone materials were used to build an 'annexe', which of course cannot now be demonstrated. He puts the date of 1500 on Gayton House. Gooch claims the building was the house of the warden of the Guild of St. Thomas, but this cannot be traced.
5. H. F. Westlake, *Parish Gilds in Medieval England*. p176.
6. 2 chapels are mentioned on the east brink – Holyrood, still there in 1517, and St. Mary on the east brink, a Chantry chapel in 1535. (*Medieval Chapels in Lincolnshire*. Dorothy Owen)
7. Sir William Rigdon (died 1610) was a Commissioner of Sewers, who lived in Dowsby and did not live in, or own, Gayton House, but alterations or 'improvements' are attributed to him by some authors.

Rough floor plan drawn during demolition. Prosser, 1959

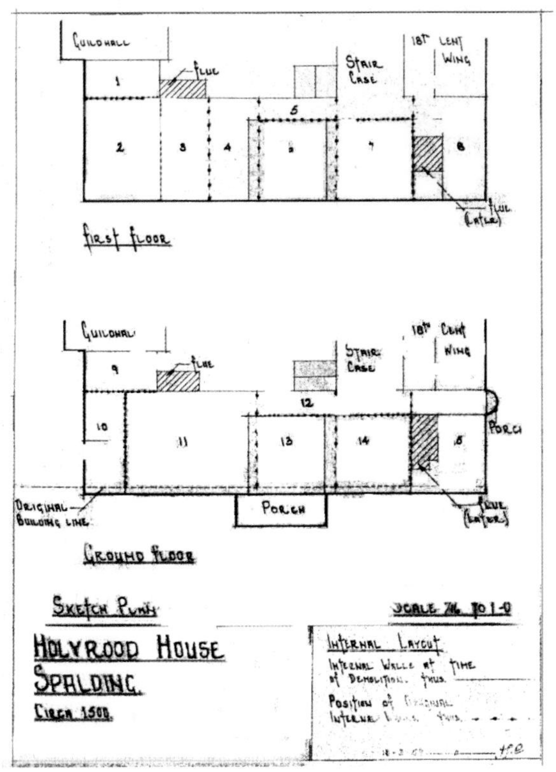

The Gayton family lived there and they probably remained there until it passed to the Hobsons. In 1684 William Ambler purchased it. William Ambler's daughter, Elizabeth, married Maurice Johnson, the Antiquary, in 1709 and afterwards on the death of her brother Joshua, she and Maurice inherited it.[1] In 1743 it was used for the meetings of the Spalding Gentlemen's Society who had leave to use the front as a physic garden. The co-adjutor[2] and his family lived in the rest of Gayton House. The Spalding Gentlemen's Society met there until 1755 when Maurice died.

Guilds were an important part of medieval life. Some were trade Guilds and some for religious purposes. In the 14th century, the religious Guild of St. John the Baptist had a chapel and altar within the Parish Church. John de Righton painted an image of St. John in 1358 which he presented to the church and in 1383 John Tovarld founded a Guild with a keeper and a chaplain to:

"*celebrate the praise of the saint [...] thirteen candles should be placed near by and funerals for the members should be attended by six candles carried by poor men or boys.*"

The Guild had no charitable purposes but no-one should be admitted unless "*the Guild deems him sufficiently good, pious and devoted.*" A fairly exclusive club

The Holy Trinity Guild was founded in 1370 when John de Toft presented an altar and 'furniture'. They were philanthropic and paid out a small sum for those members who fell into 'undeserved poverty' and had their own altars in the Parish Church.

The religious Guild of St. Mary, on the east side of the Welland, was unlike the other two because it had its own Guild house as well as an altar in the Parish Church. When Nicholas Ailwyn died in 1509 in his will there were several bequests and gifts to local Guilds, but he did not make any gift to St. Mary's. Trinity Guild and St. John's Guild[3] received £3-6-8 each from him.

He gave to the altar of St. John in the Parish Church a vestment of red worsted used by his own chaplain 'at the altar in my house.' To St. Mary's altar in the Parish Church (which he called the Lady Altar) he gives a torch[4] only.

As to the original appearance of Gayton House, the base up to the first floor level was brick (probably plastered over) and the first floor was jettied by a 2ft. overhang on the front elevation. Above was 'post and pan', timber uprights with lathes and wattle with mud and plaster between. Inside, there were carved, oak beamed ceilings[5] and several smallish rooms and the great parlour on the ground floor, 25ft. in length. This was the largest room. There was no open great hall. An unusual feature was the ground floor parlour.

---

1. Walter Johnson, Maurice the Antiquary's son, married Mary Fairfax and their son Fairfax Johnson lived there. It was after his death the house was renamed Fairfax House. For some years the two Misses Johnson, founders and benefactors of the Spalding Johnson hospital, lived there until the death of the surviving sister in 1878.
2. The co-adjutor was their name for caretaker.
3. The only other Guild he leaves a gift to are the London Cutlers, Charterhouse by Smithfield. In 1370, they were a trade Guild.
4. These torches were large candles carried in procession, and at funerals if not used up were often left in the church. Nicholas went to a lot of trouble allocating them to different altars. They were valuable commodities and weighed a much as 20lbs each.
5. One of the carved oak beams is in the possession of Spalding Gentlemen's Society. A daisy flower is carved on it.

This painting on wood is part of a panorama[1] of which - it is thought - came originally from Ayscoughfee hall. It shows both Ayscoughfee and Gayton, and it's gardens, and High Bridge. Unfortunately it is in quite bad condition, but it shows a very different frontage indeed, hardly recognisable. From the angle it is portrayed, it shows the upper storey with sash windows.[2] It is very difficult to date but may be the oldest representation of both houses and might be 17th century.

The small sketch below, of Gayton and Ayscoughfee, is taken from the Spalding Gentlemen's Society Minute Book in 1743. The house is shown with a portico and pediment and an arched doorway looking rather like the White Horse public house does now. This Inn might be the building on the far left of the sketch.

The 1743 sketch (artist unknown) shows the bay window and the front door on the far right hand side at Ayscoughfee, and Gayton looks similar to how it looks on the painted oak panel, except for the details of the fenestration.

In 1785 the front was altered again by the insertion of a Venetian window and a porch, and at about this time the roof was altered, the thatch removed and replaced with slate. The three dormer windows remain intact.

A Victorian oil painting of Gayton House, with a gas lamp on Churchgate, and is recognisably the same building as on the demolition pictures. Undated, from the SGS collection.

1. See Chapter 14
2. Dr. Hinte Louw, of the University of Newcastle Upon Tyne, suggests that the sash could have been invented earlier in the seventeenth century in England, rather than in Holland in the late seventeenth century.

Mr. Townsend[1] writes:

"The main rectangular portion (of Gayton House) looked out on the Welland with two wings, the Guildhall at the North End and an 18th century addition with staircase at the South. The Guildhall was added in the 16th century but it is not possible to ascertain what existed there prior to the 18th."

It remained a rectangular building of six bays with two wings, the north end containing the chambers of the Guild and the main south range being the Hall. The south wing would have contained the service rooms, replaced in the 18th century. This Guildhall would have been one of the most important surviving examples outside London and York, and may well be a 15th century building – and possibly earlier than Ayscoughfee.[2] The interest lies in the main building, which had many early features, stud and plaster walls, moulded oak beams, painted walls, but had been so mangled. When demolished. this wonderful opportunity to excavate and see whether the earlier building stages could be found underneath was, of course, ignored.

The layout of the original building seems unusual, two floors consisting of a number of smallish rooms, probably with only an outside staircase. As to the ground floor, the oak panelling found still in situ may well have come from Ayscoughfee. One room was painted to imitate panelling. It was too late to find any sign of the reputed painted scenes of the Priory,[3] still visible on the walls of the great parlour in the 18th century house.

Gayton had been so extensively altered over the years, that apart from the discovery of the earlier jettied front, post and pan,[4] concealed(?) brickwork, stables and outside staircase, it looked and was quite different from Ayscoughfee next door.

A hand written report made for the National Records has for the first time been procured, together with a map and photographs.

We set out Mr. M.G. Prosser's report seriatum:

"The House which was built around a rectangular courtyard with principal elevation outwards and westwards to the river. Its N and W ranges were substantially of the first half of the 16th C. The walls of the N range were of re-used ironstone ashlar (perhaps from an obsolete religious foundation) on or near the site. Those of the W range were of mixed t.f and brick construction. The S range, tho' much altered was perhaps of 17th C. origin. The E range at the time of demolition .had already been removed (it was of minor constructional consequence – domestic offices, etc. The W range was re-modelled and the interior re-modelled in the 18th C. when the staircase and staircase hall was ..... in the S W range of the ...../ The 18th C. modification to the W range entailed the almost total masking of the original work in the front of the house. As demolition proceeded the removal of Georgian ceilings in its rooms revealed in most cases. Well preserved 16th C. moulded beams and joists. The first floor as originally planned was in 6 bays of which the N most 3 were so ripped up to allow for a passageway along the E side providing access to a principal room of full width occupying the 4th and 5th bays. The 6th bay was occupied by a further, smaller room also of full width. There was an internal chimney between bays 1 & 2. The layout suggests that the 18th C staircase replaced an earlier one at about the same point. On the g.f. of the W range little investigation was possible at the dates in question. The floor boards of the g.f. rooms had been partially torn up. These were supported by rough sleeper walls made up in the main of 16th C brick & dressed lime, including a number of lengths of ogee moulded lime plaster..... and still in position at the base of N & E walls. These may have come from the W wall destroyed when the 18th C alterations were made, the indications being this, the W elevation, was originally jettied, and perhaps built in brick on the good side. It would thus have been at ground level &...... or two ...... if the 18th C W wall which was built ..... in front of the projecting upper floors."

1. Townsend's manuscript was written in 1959 at the time of the demolition. Mr. Prosser was recording architectural features for the National Buildings Record.
2. Dr Jonathan Clark
3. 'In the 16th century, on the upper walls of a parlour in a house then belonging to Mr. Gayton, since Amblers, were painted perspective views of Spalding Priory.' SGS, Minutes Vol. 4 folio 130.
4. Post and pan means timber uprights with small intervals between them. The pans being wall plates made from long sections of timber.

Top Left: Holyrood House seen from the church tower in better times.

Top right: Demolition begins at the rear.

Left: Internal partition wall showing original Elizabethan timber studwork.

Bottom: Holyrood making the headlines on Fri June 19th, 1959

Spalding Guardian

FRIDAY, JUNE 19, 1959 THREEPENCE

NO BRICKS?
BATTLEYS
CONCRETE

'discussed it'

TO
[...]CILS
[...]MEN

[...]L. COUN. W. A.
[...]ALDING RURAL
[...]O N, BOTH MADE
[...]E PRINC[...] OF

an opportune time

'Nothing more than a derelict, shapeless pile of bricks and mortar' — July 1958

CHAPTER 3

AYSCOUGHFEE HALL IN ITS SPALDING CONTEXT

The third building of the triangle, the mansion built by Richard and Nicholas Ailwyn in the middle of the 15th century, is the 'great place' of Nicholas' will and the reason for my title.

The date of 1420 has been accepted for so long but now it must be questioned. All the old traditions about the date of the building have been negated by scientific tree ring dating, firmly dating the wood. The roof timbers were nearly all felled in 1451 or thereabouts, which suggests that the building was completed in the early 1450s.

Ayscoughfee was not built in a day and would certainly have taken several years. As Richard (or whoever designed it) planned it as a whole unit to be built all together, it was a large project needing a considerable capital and a large labour force. The plan was for a traditional central hall with cross wings and a great hall open to the roof with a hearth in the centre. The north cross wing had a smaller hall with a chamber above. In the tower, the main bedroom. A garderobe adjoined it. There is a floor above. The south cross wing was for services. The south cross wing comprised the outside kitchen, service rooms and guest accommodation. A fine staircase with a vaulted brick ceiling led to this, which would impress any visitor. Walled up, invisible for years, this staircase is now revealed, with the brickwork almost in the pristine condition it was when built. The pinkish brick ceiling is finely vaulted and very beautiful.

The size of the building, the guest accommodation and the great tower demonstrates the affluence of the Ailwyn family and their desire to impress. Had they seen Tattershall, (pictured left) Lord Cromwell's establishment built in 1434-50? Had they heard of Bishop Waynefleet's[2] building projects? The gatehouse at Thornton Abbey was built of brick before Tattershall, a splendid and impressive place, built in 1382 of stone and brick by the then Abbott, with its ground floor hall, oriel windows, vaulted staircase with turrets and archways.

Samuel & Nathaniel Buck's Tattershall Castle, first published in 1760

These buildings would have had a deep effect on the Ailwyns. Thornton, with three floors, arches and small round towers, the massive Tattershall tower with ornamental brick and four corner octagonal turreted towers[3] giving an impression of massive splendour. Gainsborough Old Hall was also being built, and had a grand tower and a large bay window.

After 1451 Nicholas travelled regularly making the journey from Spalding to London, which would have opened his eyes to the grand London churches and mansions. Was it Nicholas' influence that persuaded his father to adopt some of the new ideas? And they were new; the use of brick would have surprised the Spalding inhabitants.

---

1. Henry III gave 100 oaks to Spalding Priory to renovate their conventual church, brought all the way from Rockingham. Ayscoughfee, with its extensive roofs, would have taken as many.
2. Bishop Waynefleet was a Lincolnshire man, born in Wainfleet in 1395. He was responsible for Oxford's Magdalen College and many other brick buildings. Mr. Gooch's fertile imagination is not reliable here as Bishop Waynefleet had nothing to do with Spalding.
3. Now only the keep of Tattershall remains. The tower was for living purposes, although it looks defensive. It was built of brick and stone.

At about the same time that the Ailwyns, father and son, were contemplating their grand design, across the river in Spalding Priory a map-making monk was drawing careful sketches of churches in the locality for a sketch plan, which has only been recognised recently as 15th century.

The Pinchbeck Fen map[1] (left) shows the River Welland and the bridge over it; on the west side the church of the Priory is portrayed and on the east the Parish Church. The artist seemed to be familiar with the churches he portrayed and drew accurate features which can still be recognised.

The Parish Church (shown right) with its spire (including the south porch, built in 1360), shows the chapel built by Richard Skinner, with a little round tower, now disappeared, but substantially the same recognisable building, which the Ailwyns would have known so well, and to which they were benefactors.

The Priory Church (left; with a cockerel weathervane) was over High Bridge, and is shown in detail on the Map; with the wide entrance way, a large spire and a sweep of drive. Unfortunately, the Priors' Oven[2] is not the building shown near the Great Gate at the end of the Gore. The site of the Priory is roughly behind the row of shops, running from Priors' Oven, through into Hall Place and behind Boots and Burtons. In the Sheep Market - until 1852 – the boundary remained as part of the former storehouses and granary of the Priory, along the line of the old Post Office (now a bookmakers) at the corner of the lane called Gore Lane.[3] On an early postcard of the Priors' Oven, the lane running behind it is marked as Malting House Square.

The Pinchbeck map does not include secular buildings but two of the Priory granges are shown (Monks House) and somewhere called *Nova Aula* (New Hall). It gives the view of the Priory that would have been familiar to the Ailwyns; before this map was discovered the exact appearance of the Priory Church was not known.

Spalding Priory was not at the peak of its fame during the 15th century. In fact it was not at all its golden hour; when Bishop Alnwick came for his visitation in 1438 he found much amiss and things were not much improved by the next visitation in 1519 by Bishop Atwater.

---

1. *The Pinchbeck Fen Map* published by Imago Mundi Ltd. Rose Mitchell and David Crook. Dated probably mid-15th century, perhaps 1445-50.
2. Now thankfully restored with great care from a ruinous condition, it was about to fall down through neglect. It was entirely funded by private enterprise.
3. Gore Lane is not now prominently marked. The way into Abbey Yard is now called Bedford Place and is now mostly car park, but Abbey Passage remains marked as such. Gooch quotes Stukeley from an address to the Society of Antiquaries, about the "great mitred priory of Spalding", and this where the various "abbey" street names originate.

As to the priors, the century opens with Prior John of Moulton (1404-21) followed by Robert Holland (1421-1438), William of Pinchbeck (1444-1453) and Thomas of Spalding[1] (1453-1475). Their dates are not exactly clear and accounts vary.[2] Thomas of Moulton was Prior from 1475 onwards. The Bishop's visitation of August 1438/9 reveal much that was unsatisfactory in the time of Prior Robert Holland when the Bishop found neglect, pressing creditors, the poor not being fed and wages to secular servants not being paid, 'women' being let in and wine being sold in the monastery. He died the same year.[3]

There seems little to connect the Ailwyns with Spalding Priory. None of the family were buried there, as far as can be traced. Both Richard and Margaret's graves are at the Parish Church, while Nicholas who died in London is buried at St. Mary le Bow. His will includes some small gifts to the Priory.

Spalding was then a busy port but commerce was concentrated on the other side of High Bridge. The east brink was not densely populated, but the larger houses were on this side. The building of Ayscoughfee must have taken some years to complete during Nicholas' young manhood. When he came to make his will he was remembering those days Nicholas mentions Whitehead of Stanground in his will, leaving him a £5 legacy, as the 'carrier of my timber to Spalding.' This may be a reference to the building of the house. With him is remembered three other carpenters, Buntying (£5), John Bankes (£5) and Stephen of Tanglin (£5). These bequests come after the gifts to his household and no other artisans who could have been involved in building the house are mentioned or remembered. Nicholas would have remembered the felling, seasoning and sawing up of the massive oak trees, all done by hand by these craftsmen. Then they would have to be transported by horse and cart to Spalding, and a great many trees would have been set aside and earmarked for this project.[4] Nicholas' special legacy to three carpenters reflects the very weary and arduous work they undertook and Nicholas' remembrance is appreciation of it.

But the great innovation for the Ailwyn project was the use of bricks throughout the building, quite a novelty in the mid-15th century. Handmade, often made on the spot if the soil conditions were clay and suitable for brick making, they were small and pinkish with darker colouring. There was a brick-making industry at this time in Hull. Tattershall is the nearest place they might have visited and seen bricks in use. The building there went on between 1434-1440. There were four storeys, a Hall and chambers, one on each floor and four crenellated turrets, which gave the building a great splendour; decorated brick with some stone edging for the windows, octagonal towers dotted with lots of windows, turrets topped with pointed caps, all of brick. The art of brick-making had been known for centuries; the Romans made them and mixed them with the stone as in the Mint Wall in Lincoln. The Saxon church at Brixworth re-used some Roman brick and stone. The practice fell into disuse, although it was still sometimes used in Suffolk.

The attention to detail is demonstrated by the unusual ribbed vaulting of the staircase in the south range at Ayscoughfee (left).

1. *Spalding Priory (1052-2000)*, William Snowdon, 2003
2. The exact dates are lost for this period because in 1467 there were terrible floods all over Holland and the Civil Wars of the Roses were raging between 1455-1485. No-one seems to agree the prior's dates (Thomas of Moulton), 1472-90 and there is no established list of vicars for this period.
3. Robert Holland is said to have built the north porch of the Parish Church. On the brighter side, Geoffrey Chaucer was a regular visitor to the Priory.
4. Probably the wood was roughly prepared and numbered off site, and then transported. Much of it would have to be sawn into planks for roof and floor timbers. Elm wood was used for some floors.
5. In 1382, Thornton Abbey was first, then Kirby Muxloe's moated castle in Leicestershire in 1480 was built of brick; the master mason was John Cowper of Tattershall.

During the 15th century red bricks came back into fashion and Ayscoughfee was an early example; it seems the first domestic example in Spalding's district.[1]

Tattershall Keep, made of red brick, was completed in 1440 by the Lord Treasurer, Lord Cromwell,[2] and was part of a large complex of buildings surrounded by a double moat. The Keep was designed as a large dwelling house, a massive height of 112 feet, with thick walls, 16-22ft. overall. The impression is of military strength but there are indications that this was only to impress. The windows are large, too large to be defensible, but were obviously intended to make the whole building comfortably light. It would easily accommodate one hundred people. As he was an unpopular minister, he may have wanted it to appear impregnable, to provide himself with a safe house if he was ever attacked.

Above: Hussey Tower, Boston in 1815.

It is the use of bricks that make Tattershall a useful comparison with Ayscoughfee. Some of the accounts have survived. The clerks of works who supervised the master mason and his men, 'freestone masons', supplied 322,000 bricks (called large tiles)[3] for the building of the donjon[4] (great tower) at Tattershall. The brick kilns were at Edlington Moor and the bricks made by one Baldwin. The overall design was to the master's while the master craftsmen interpreted his ideas and the clerk of the works supervised. Architects and their names are not known, but are possibly John Cowper the mason, or Peter Lyndon. Regrettably, nothing is known about the actual building of Ayscoughfee.

Richly coloured Medieval builders under close supervision

1. The Hussey Tower, built by Richard Benyngton in around the 1440s and now in ruins, was the home of Lord Hussey, executed for his alleged part in the Pilgrimage of Grace in 1538. It is of red brick, three floors high, square in plan with crenellated parapets. The Rochford Tower in Skirbeck is very similar with three floors, turrets and a parapet, and built around the 1450s.
2. Ralph, 3rd Baron Cromwell (died 1456).
3. Brick layers were 'tilers', who worked on the masonry as well as the 'wall tiles'.
4. *Tattershall Castle.* The National Trust 1965.

CHAPTER 4

THE AILWYN FAMILY

Who were the Ailwyns? Clearly recognisable through so many different spellings, they were ALDWYN, AILWIN, ALEWYNE or even HALEWYNE. For consistency, I have used Ailwyn throughout the book, but Aldwyn is equally correct. By a strange coincidence the very first 'mayor' of London in 1189 was Henry Fitz-Ailwyn[1] known as the Portreeve of London; he is well documented and died a very rich man after holding the post for twenty years.

Nicholas Ailwyn of Spalding was Lord Mayor of London in 1499, holding the office for the normal one year. It would be fanciful to seek a connection with the first Ailwyns. Nicholas had more in common with Dick Whittington[2] who made the long journey from the provinces to make his fortune in London with his cat for company.

As to Nicholas Ailwyn's background, his parents Richard and Margaret Ailwyn are the first recorded Ailwyns of Spalding. Nothing is known of their lives, except that they lived in and are buried in Spalding and were both dead by 1505. Their son Nicholas was probably born in about 1435 and there may have been other children.

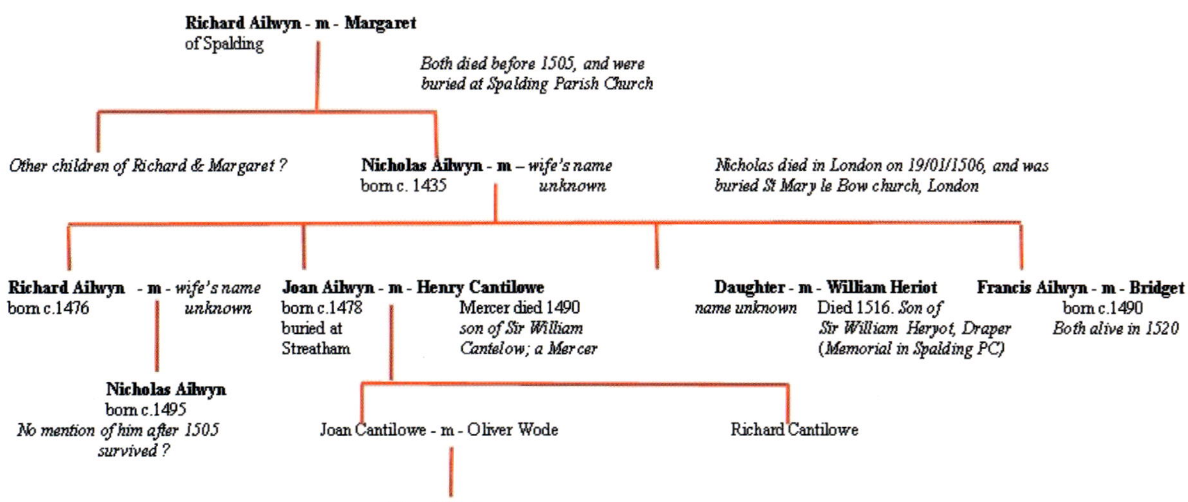

Traditionally, old Richard is thought to be a wool merchant who was very successful in his trade. Despite claims he was Sir Richard, there is no evidence he was knighted, or that he was involved in politics. He was almost certainly a Merchant of the Staple. He was a hard working, ambitious but strongly independent merchant; the kind of man the Fenlanders have always produced.

---

1. It was a royal appointment and so unelected; his son followed him into office.
2. Sir Richard Whittington came from a provincial background in Gloucestershire, was apprenticed to a mercer and became Mayor of London four times 1396 & 98, 1406 & 19. He left his vast fortune to found many charitable institutions on his death in 1423.

His life's work is the house he built for himself and his family, Ayscoughfee Hall, now dated firmly by tests on the roof timber. The timber rings give a date for felling of 1451. The wood would have to be seasoned before it was used, probably for several years. The date of 1420, always accepted, has now to be put forward to allow for seasoning and the time taken over building, giving a date of around 1451 or slightly later.

The Ailwyn family business was in wool and the probability is they were involved in wool exporting. Nearby, 15th century Boston was a centre for the international wool trade dominated by the Merchants of the Staple and the great annual fair of St. Botolph. In the 13th century the wool trade was at its peak and Boston was the second largest port after London. Although trade had declined and was still declining, Boston was still an important centre for wool in Nicholas' day and had a complicated system of customs, keeping detailed accounts for every port from Hull to Kings Lynn. All wool had to go to the market staple at Calais and the Merchants of the Staple, a powerful national company, had a firm grip of the market both in England and France. Many merchants owned their own ships but there is no evidence that the Ailwyns had ships and no information about their trading in Spalding has been found.

Whatever the source, to build a house of the size and grandeur of 'the Great Place' meant enormous expenditure. It was built all in one piece, not piecemeal, a large custom-built mansion designed to house a prosperous man and his family and a place to conduct his business from and to impress his neighbours and customers. Built in the new fashioned brick, it was carefully planned and designed with every convenience, including a large guest suite on the first floor.

Over the door, where the guests would have entered, is a round stone plaque (which is thought to be in the original place where it was installed). All sorts of crazy conjectures have been made as to what it represents. It is now worn by the elements but enough remains to make out the figures. It is possibly an introduction to the household, showing the hosts and informing visitors the nature of the hospitality they were soon to be offered. A family group; old Richard Ailwyn sits in an armchair wearing the felt hat of a merchant. He has a long beard and bushy eyebrows. Margaret, his wife, was not present and must have died. To demonstrate his importance he is being served 'on the knee' by a 'page' who is handing out small cakes.

The second, younger, man, also bearded, is eating; he looks proud and cheerful as if the cakes or doughnuts please him; he is like his father in face and figure. He also wears a beaver hat, but of a different kind, with a bigger crown. This might be his son, Nicholas. Both are big built and sturdy looking. Next to him is a woman with a large and heavy hat, like a turban, wound round her head and tied. Her dress is long and pleated and just above her ankles, and her arms and hands are very worn but she too might be eating something. It is reminiscent of Geoffrey Chaucer's reference to a lady's headgear.[1] This lady might be Nicholas' wife. The fourth, smaller figure must be a child; he has his chin on his mother's shoulder, he is clumsily carved and very worn; he might be carrying a toy sword or be wearing a long skirt, but it is obviously a boy-child and not a servant being familiar with his mistress.
Is this one of the grandchildren. Richard, perhaps?

Roundel: Wendy Nix

1. Canterbury Tales by Geoffrey Chaucer describes the wife of Bath as wearing on her head 'coverchiefs full fine', on Sunday 'he could swear they weighed ten pounds.'

This roundel could therefore be an introduction to the family. A very sensible idea then, when most of the population could not read. A sensible idea now, helping to put names to faces. As to their clothes, the two beaver hats, one with a small brim and one with a cord or ribbon and a larger brim, were fashionable throughout Henry VI's reign, 1422-61. Both men have full beards and moustaches which may have made them stand out. The young man on his one knee wears a belted, pleated cotehardie, almost a frill on the hips with a wide, tight belt and tights. Although the shoes are worn they look pointed, not altogether blunt. He is bare-headed and has wide sleeves and short hair as far as can be seen. The woman's gown is ankle length and belted with narrow sleeves. This may reflect her domestic life. Skirts were extremely long at this date for grand ladies. Her head is covered by what looks like a turban, a fashion in 1453 after the fall of Constantinople, when turbans were fashioned by padding a roll of velvet silk or cloth, usually decorated with ropes of pearls or brooches. Turbans remained fashionable after 1460, but the one she wears is very plain indeed and she has no veil or other adornment. Her shoes look sensibly rounded. She is perhaps portrayed as a housewife and not a grand lady. Ladies' clothes were very showy and elaborate at this time. The figure in long clothes is not very expertly carved but it must be a young child.

Old Richard and his wife Margaret may have had several children and there is no clue to her identity nor the date of her death, or to the death of her unnamed daughter-in-law.

Old Richard built Ayscoughfee Hall probably between 1450-1460, a most expensive and ambitious project, perhaps on a site where there was already a house.[1] Old Richard, as portrayed in the roundel, looks benevolently contented. He smiles benignly out, proud of his house, his position and his family. He had plans for his son Nicholas, and did not wish him to follow him into the business immediately without seeing the world and London. Whether old Richard was a Mercer is unknown but in the course of business he must have come across the company. Richard was a Merchant of the Staple. He apprenticed Nicholas to the great Mercers Company who operated from London, which meant Nicholas would leave home for his apprenticeship. John Brodisworth was chosen as his master, with whom he probably lived with at first. Nicholas, just sixteen, started his apprenticeship in 1451[2] (and it officially lasted for 10 years) then afterwards spent most of his life in London acquiring property there but returning to Spalding periodically.

"Les Très Riches Heures"
A banquet in a French manuscript made for Jean, Duc de Berry in the early fifteenth century. A very grand affair with guests wearing the height of fashion, entertaining a Prelate. The Duc himself wears a blue gown and fur hat. Note the servants with lace towels, and the puppies on the table. There are no ladies present.

1. Maurice Johnson, the Antiquary, considered there was an earlier house there.
2. Extracted from The Mercers Wardens Accounts Book 1391-1464

When Nicholas was married is not known but his wife survived long enough to produce four children, the youngest in 1495. She gave birth to Joan, who married Henry, the son of Sir William Cantelowe,[1] a mercer, one of the Cantelowe family, who died in 1490. When Nicholas' will was being written by William Carkeke, the scrivener, Nicholas could not remember his daughter's name referring to her as "my daughter called Cantelowe". He remembered she was buried in Streatham Church and leaves a fund for candles to be set about "my daughter's tomb every Easter as long as the money lasts".

Joan's daughter, his granddaughter also called Joan, is later referred to as Joan Wode; she is also remembered in Nicholas's will and her husband Oliver who appears to be part of his household.

The mysterious son Richard, the eldest, is not mentioned except as "Richard my son, father of Nicholas".[2] Maybe Richard was already dead by 1505.[£] Nicholas remembers where his grandson Nicholas was born in the parish of Blechingley in 1495. He does not mention his son Richard at all. Nicholas, the grandson, was eleven at the time of the will.

The Luttrell Psalter Banquet: Earlier than Ayscoughfee (c.1340), the banquet shown here is a simple and more countrified affair, but still demonstrates how the High Table is furnished. Sir Geoffrey Luttrell, his wife and guests are being attended to by their butler John, and a servant (with a towel over his shoulder) serving them 'on the knee'.

1. The Cantelowes produced several generations of mercers (see p328 of Appendix to *The Merchant Class of Medieval London*)
2. *The Merchant Class of Medieval London*, Sylvia Thrupp. 1948. University of Chicago Press. p328.
3. A small carving of a youth dressed as an apprentice, in Spalding Parish Church, with a stretched imagination might be a reference to Richard who died before completion of his apprenticeship. He is carrying a harp.

The son, Richard was apprenticed to his father in 1491 and must have been sixteen at the time. Another daughter married a Heriot, or Heryot, a member of a leading merchant family of London. He was William Heriot, draper, son of Sir William Hereyot, an Alderman. Nicholas' two sons in law, William Heriot and Richard Cantelowe, were close enough to be involved together in many business deals. (There was a memorial to William Heriot in Spalding Parish Church with the Ailwyn coat of arms, now disappeared.[1])

If this pew end (left) is Richard's memorial, the gothic harp in his arms may not have heavenly connotations. It was, perhaps, his hobby.

The image on the right shows an angel from the "Angel Choir" at Lincoln Cathedral also playing a Gothic harp, which has a carrying case, like the one held by Richard. It was a very popular instrument in the 15th century.

The following carvings further show the popularity of the harp in church decoration.

Left, a twelfth century fox entertaining a dancer at Barfreston, Kent

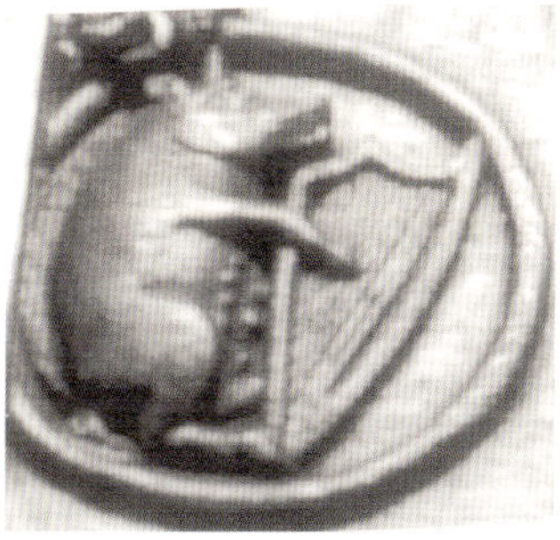

Right, a 16th century misericord at Manchester Cathedral shows a 12-string harp being played by a pig.

1. The memorial described him as merchant of London and Parma. See Holles. SC/C1380-46. Holles' reference to this memorial is unambiguous and means he was importing fabrics. The date of his death is unknown. It is clear that his connection with the Ailwyn family had survived until his death.

Norwich Cathedral roof bosses:
The very smart, contemporary, 15th century angel (on the far left) is carrying a torch. The image on the right shows the medieval way of death: The small children being ushered into Heaven by two female angels shows the mastery of the stonemason who carved this boss at Norwich Cathedral.

Francis, or Fraunceys, was under 21 in 1505. Unlike his elder brother Richard he was not apprenticed to the Mercers; he became his father's heir after Richard's death as his only surviving son. He married Bridget and they lived in his father's house in London until his death in the late 1520s. They sold and divided much of the family's London property retaining "Francis Ailwyn's great house in Bow Churchyard". In 1515 Francis Ailwyn was involved in litigation and described himself as a Mercer and appears to be in debt. His wife, Bridget, sold three houses in Bow for payments of his debts and they let the "great house in Bow" and lived off the rent. More research is needed to find whether Nicholas, the next heir, had survived by the time of the death of Francis, but it appears he did not

But it can now be shown that Francis survived and lived in his father's London house, but whether he ever lived in Spalding, or took any interest in it, is as yet unknown. After about 1530 the trail goes cold, so it appears that the Ailwyns died with Francis and that the house passed into other hands.[1] This crucial gap is tantalizing. In 1556 Reginald Hall inherited Ayscoughfee from his mother[1] so the gap between the probable date of Francis Ailwyn's death and Reginald Hall's inheritance is only 30 years, or less.

1. See reference to Juliana Roberts Hall in Chapter 11

CHAPTER 5

THE DE GAYTON FAMILY

Some documents relating to the Gayton house and occupants must have survived for Mr. Gooch to see in 1940 because he refers to the occupants as "Domina Isabella Gayton[1] and Reginald Gayton Generosus." He gives no source. He does not claim that the Gayton family built it and it may have been there before them. There is no contemporary information on the Gayton family's presence there and no mention of the name 'Isabella'.

Gayton Manor House & St Mary's Church, (Northants)

Of the three places called Gayton in the locality, Gayton Thorpe[2] in Norfolk is an ancient village with a Saxon church. Gayton-le-Marsh[3] is a tiny village near the Lincolnshire coast, with an old church and some connection with Queen Edith, but no famous families. Gayton in Northamptonshire[4] is more rewarding. It was the seat of the Gayton family who are quite well documented and seem to disappear without trace in the 15th century. It must be made plain that there is no direct link with the Gayton family who are said to have built and lived in Gayton House, Spalding in 1480, but my hypothesis fits.

The de Gayton family emerges in the twelfth and thirteenth centuries as a knightly family, owners of an estate in Gayton, Northamptonshire. It was part of the ancient Honor of Chokes, which by 1160 belonged to the family of the Hereditary Advocate, the Bethunes.[5] It passed through various families and came into the hands of Michael de Houghton de Northampton. His brother John followed in 1270. In 1271 the manor was split off from the rest of the land[6] and Juliana, the only daughter of John de Houghton, inherited it and married into a local family. They adopted the name of the village where they lived before the age of surnames. Such was the origin of the de Gaytons; Juliana's son, Sir Philip de Gayton, has a very grand, imposing tomb in the Gayton Parish Church (left). The effigy is unusual in that it is wooden and shows him wearing armour, a sword at his side and a dog at his feet. He has crossed legs which some interpret as a sign that he might have been a Crusader.
He died in 1316.

The oak effigy of Sir Philip de Gayton

Of Sir Philip's children, his heir Theobald only survived him by a few days, leaving a widow Margery but no children. His two sisters were sole heiresses of his estates. This is probably the reason why he is known as the 'last of the Gaytons.'

1. Alderman E. Gooch, *History of Spalding*. p111. This is the only reference to Isabella.
2. Near Kings Lynn, Norfolk.
3. Near Mablethorpe.
4. A few miles from Northampton, near Blisworth.
5. His inquisition post-mortem
6. The present Gayton manor house is Elizabethan.

Juliana and Scholastica were in their twenties. Scholastica married Sir Godfrey de Meaux[1] and Juliana's husband was Sir Thomas Murdak. Scholastica's husband was Lord of Gayton in right of his wife. They had many other possessions.

By the end of the year disaster had struck her sister and Thomas. Murdak was dead. Regrettably, it was discovered that Juliana had murdered him. She was duly convicted of this. In 1316 she was publicly burnt[2] and all her property escheated to her overlord. It was suggested that she was involved with another man, John Vaux. She was convicted of petty treason.[3]

Her share was first forfeited, then granted to her sister, Scholastica, who now had a son called John who inherited the whole manor on his mother's death in 1354. After the death of John de Meaux in 1377 the Trussell family inherited and the de Gaytons were not mentioned after 1377, the date of his will. There is no further trace of them.

In the Gayton Parish Church a life-size tomb commemorates Lady Scholastica (left). She has a rather plain face and is wearing a long gown and mantle and she holds the cord of it in her left hand. A paris hood is falling to her shoulders and there is a small fillet round her head revealing a neat centre parting. The very long skirt and the cords and tassels are 14th century. Her dress is so long that it rolls over her feet which rest on a very fierce lion.

Another de Gayton, Mabila, is shown on a tiny 18" stone memorial, a small girl who died in the 14th century, but she has two coats of arms on her tiny head cushion.[4] She was probably the daughter of Thomas de Gayton.

Mabila's memorial: The inscription reads "hic jacet in tumba Mabila, filia Thome de ... "

The two Gayton coats of arms are:

Johan de Gayton: "*with argent a fess between six fleur de lis gules.*"

Sir Phillip: "*argent crusilly and three fleur de lis azure.*"

In 1504 the manor was held by the hospital of St. John of Jerusalem, the Gayton family having died out. There is mention of Phillip de Gayton, a Thomas and a William de Gayton in the time of Bishop Dalderby[5] of Lincoln. There were several de Gaytons at this time and they could have settled in Spalding.

1. Meaux, sometimes Melce, Melsa or Meux. Bridges. *History of Northampton*. Vol. I p262-263
2. Baker, *History of Northampton*. Vol. 3 p275
3. There was nothing petty about petty treason; the only punishment was death by burning.
4. Described by Arthur Mee. *The King's England, Northamptonshire* 1945
5. A register compiled in the time of Edward III of all the Knights of England. Baker. Vol. III, p27.

CHAPTER 6

THE AYSCOUGHS

The family of Ayscough[1] has ancient origins but they are not in Lincolnshire. Their pedigree is contentious and takes up sixteen pages of Maddison's Lincolnshire Pedigrees. This family produced a protestant martyr, a murdered archbishop, an author, a Commissioner of Sewers, an Antiquarian, an Admiral, a Customs Officer and several county sheriffs. What it did not produce was any evidence of any Ayscough living in Spalding. Any link to Ayscoughfee would have to be before the known sequence of conveyancing documents[2] which starts in 1602. Thereafter the preserved conveyances are sequential and there are no gaps - between 1602 and 1898 when Isabella Johnson, the widow of the last Johnson, gave the property to the citizens of Spalding.

However, the Ayscoughs must be examined before they are finally excluded as owners of Ayscoughfee Hall. They seem to have origins in Lacra, near Millom in Cumberland and to have moved to Lincolnshire in the 16th century. Once in Blyborough they moved up the social ladder, Sir Henry Ayscough being knighted in 1603 at Whitehall at the same time as his son Walter. Ayscoughs inter-married into the Dymoke family (1592), the Harringtons (Exton and Ridlington, Rutland) 1611-1633, and the family of Pennington (Muncaster, Cumberland) 1563. There is also an inter-marriage with a relation of Charles Brandon, Duke of Suffolk of Grimsthorpe, Lincolnshire and elsewhere.

The Stallingborough Ayscough coat of arms is distinctive. "*Argent a fesse between three asses passant sable. Blyborough, the same with a crescent difference of the last.*" This canting[3] became known as the "coughing asses", giving clues as to the proper pronunciation of Ayscough. The Ayscoughs of Stallingborough and South Kelsey appear to be the senior branch and emanate from Durham, Yorkshire (according to Maddison) while Walter Conway claims they descend from Thurstan de Bosco in a place called Aiksheugh, at Millom, Cumberland, in the time of King John. In the time of Edward III, in the 13th century, this family bought Pott Grange, Yorkshire and produced four Richards and three Williams. In 1457 William Asquith was recorded as "keeper of the Abbot's Cattle" (Fountains Abbey) at Pott Grange. Perhaps this was a grander occupation than it seemed. Their fortunes were rising.

A William Ayscough became Bishop of Salisbury in Henry VI's time and during the Jack Cade rising in 1450 was barbarously murdered by a mob. Another Sir William Ayscough became a Justice of Common Pleas and was discontented; he complained of his loss of fees when made a judge and pleaded with the King "to give him for his life certain tenements".

---

1. Ayscough, Ayscoghe, Aiscough, Askew, Askewe, Ascue, Ascu, Eascue, even Asquith. Rev'd. J. Walter Conway. *The Ayscough family and their connections*. Pamphlet in possession of the Spalding Gentlemen's Society, 1896.
2. The first known use of the name Ayscough in a deed for the house by an owner is contained in the 1602 conveyance, when Robert Hall sold 'my manor of Aiscough'. The Valor Ecclesiastatius in 1536 refers to the 'fee of Askehughe'.
3. A heraldic joke.

He complained he was losing his sight and was the "poorest of all your Justices". But he continued for fourteen years. In 1448 he was given the Hospital of St. Nicholas at Richmond. He married well, an heiress called Elizabeth Cathorpe or Caythorp of Ergham. Their son George married Alice, sister of Sir Christopher Wray of Glentworth, Chief Justice of the King's Bench, a well known Lincolnshire family.

This was the first link with Lincolnshire, but still the family had no Lincolnshire base.

Following the chronicles of the Ayscoughs, now comes the only possible connection with Spalding, the inter-marriages of the Ayscoughs with the Taillbois family. Ivo Taillbois was given the Manor of Spalding by William I, the Conqueror. He was the builder of Spalding Castle and was much hated by his tenants as a Norman bully. He married Lucy, whose pedigree is still a puzzle. They were both generous benefactors to the Priory. The Taillbois family settled in Stallingborough and became anglicised as Taillboys, but as there are several branches it cannot be established that Sir Henry Taillboys[1] Knight, Lord of Kyme, who acquired the title upon marriage to the heiress of William of Kyme, Margaret, was a descendant of the original Frenchman. Margaret Taillboys was a great heiress. She inherited from her father, John Taillboys of Stallingborough. She was sole heir of her mother (a Gibthorpe) and her grandmother (a Cokefield of Nuthall, Nottinghamshire). She was also connected with Robert Charnells and was his heir. Despite extensive searches no trace of any part of her estates can be found in South Lincolnshire. Her children were Edward, Elizabeth and William, later Sir William, Sheriff of Lincoln who died in 1509 and was buried in Stallingborough Parish Church with his wife, Margery Hildyard. Both have brasses in Stallingborough church, she wearing her armorial bearings on her very long gown, he is in armour.

Margaret Taillboys brought all her estates to John Ayscough when she married and he became Lord of Stallingborough. Little is known of her. She was 21 in 1467 and her father's sole heir, which meant her husband became Lord of Stallingborough,[2] Lord of the Manor of Nuthall and Basford in Nottingham, on marriage. Sir John Cockfield[3] and Richard Foljambe, her relatives, agreed that Margaret should have 'all the lands' if she had no male heirs, the remainder would go 'to others'. No details of the date of the marriage or Margaret's death have survived but of her three Ayscough children, Edward, Elizabeth and William, Edward had a son, Robert, living in 1540 and a daughter, Anne, who married Thomas Portington. Nothing is known of Elizabeth who married William (or Thomas) Booth of Killingholme, Lincolnshire. They appear to be the end of the line. Sir William was knighted by Henry VIII and was Sheriff of Lincolnshire in 1500, 1505 and 1508 and died in 1509. Presumably, he inherited Margaret's fortune.

The brasses in Stallingborough Parish Church (one now concealed by a carpet) show Margery with a kennel head-dress, hands clasped, wearing a highly ornamental belt low on her hips and a robe with heraldic designs, flowing round her feet, her round toes just peeping out.

Sir William is depicted in chain plate armour, his feet enclosed in round toed armoured shoes, his sword hangs behind him and he too has heraldic emblems on his armour. He was Anne Askew's grandfather. She was the protestant martyr in 1546.

1. George Taillbois had acquired from the Wellby family of Moulton (Thomas Wellby died in 1493) some manors and lands in South Holland. He was Sir George, Knight of Kyme and High Sheriff of Lincolnshire in the 1496 inquisition, but this connection is too late to be relevant.
2. The family then settled in Stallingborough and became Ayscough of Stallingborough and South Kelsey. Maddison, p60.
3. Sir John Cockfield was Lord of the Manor of Nuthall, just outside Nottingham.

Some of this heraldry is repeated on a grand memorial for a later Ayscough.

Sir Edward Ayscough (who died in 1612) and his wife Hester (left) and their many children are shown on a tomb slab (below).

Another memorial shows the head and shoulders of Sir Francis Ayscough (below), topped by a full coat of arms (shown at the beginning of the chapter).

He was born in 1508 and died in 1564 and was buried at South Kelsey. His arms were: "*quarterly, sable a fesse or between three asses passant argent, maned and unguled of the second.*"

The Commissioner of Sewers for Lincolnshire, Francis Ayscough, was appointed in 1547 and does not appear to have any connection with Spalding. The canting nature of this coat of arms, referred to as the 'coughing donkey' (Ass-cough!) is obviously very much an Ayscoughfee trade mark and they used it whenever possible. The asses are on the floor brass and feature distinctly round the neck of the armour. It is difficult to believe that a family joke of this kind should not have been inscribed somewhere in Ayscoughfee Hall, if the Ayscoughs ever lived there as their home.

None of this family heraldry can be found in Spalding in general or Ayscoughfee in particular, and I can find no more relevant marriages. There is no sign of an Ayscough presence in the Spalding Parish Church. Explanations must be sought elsewhere. If they were too grand for the Parish Church and were buried in the Priory, no records remain. But the Ayscoughs, if they ever lived in Ayscoughfee Hall, left no trace. I am not breaking new ground in claiming the Ayscoughs were not the owners or builders of Ayscoughfee, this conclusion was reached by the Reverend J. Walter Conway,[1] writing in 1896, who undertook a history of the Ayscough family, dealing in great detail with every branch. He put forward an idea that an Ayscough might have been a steward of Spalding Priory but could find nothing to support this (p.23). He also points out the connection with the Hussey family. Lord Hussey was High Steward of Spalding at the time of the Lincolnshire uprising. William Ayscough was then a steward of Thornton Abbey. Lord Hussey lost his head as he was found to have been involved, but William Ayscough survived. In 1896, Conway's conclusion was that although there were local connections with the county, there is no evidence at all to link the Ayscoughs with Ayscoughfee Hall. But there is no present proposal to change its name to Ailwyn Hall.

1. See Walter Conway's pamphlet. An explanation for the name lies elsewhere.

CHAPTER 7

NICHOLAS AILWYN'S CAREER WITH THE MERCERS

The life span of Richard Ailwyn and his son bridged the 15th century. Richard was probably born near the beginning, while Nicholas survived into the new century, dying in 1506. This century was a time of upheaval from the time Henry Bolingbroke usurped the throne in 1399 becoming Henry IV, until Richard III was defeated at Bosworth by Henry VII in 1485, who became the first Tudor, reigning when Nicholas was Lord Mayor of London in 1499

The country was struggling with civil wars and wars with France, and yet the Ailwyns thrived and became sufficiently prosperous to afford to build a high-status house and to own much property by the middle of the century. Richard Ailwyn always kept a low profile; he probably laid the foundations of the family business, but almost nothing is known of his life except that he and his wife were dead by 1506 and were buried in Spalding. No-one can say whether his father before him was also a merchant or whether the family had Lincolnshire origins. Richard was not mentioned in the lists of Mercers. As for Richard's son, if it was not for the records kept by the Mercers Company[1] much less would be known about the life of Nicholas Ailwyn. As it is, their records trace his life and progress from apprentice to Lord Mayor of London. The Mercers, a livery company of London, were a guild or trade association with very early beginnings as old as the word 'guild' (from Saxon 'gild' – to pay), and as old as the idea of merchants gathering together with traders and shopkeepers for the protection of their interests. The Mercers were incorporated in 1394. As the Mercers played such an important part in Nicholas' life a little more about them would be helpful. The Worshipful Company of Mercers records go back to 1348 but the company is first mentioned in about 1190. It is one of the twelve Livery Companies of the City of London, trade associations for merchants. The Mercers were usually wool merchants like the later Merchants of the Staple; first incorporated by Royal Charter in 1394. Throughout its existence as a gild or fraternity for many years, it used as its emblem a girl's head, always referred to as 'the Maiden' or 'the Maidenhead'[2].

When the company was finally officially granted arms in 1568, the Maidenhead was the focal point and the coat of arms was described as; "*Gules, a demi-virgin couped below the shoulders issuing from clouds all proper vested or crowned with an Eastern crown of the last her hair dishevelled and wreathed round the temples with roses of the second all within an orle of clouds in proper.*"

---

1. *An Account of the Mistery of Mercers of the City of London*. Sir John Watney, London 1914. (Mistery from the Latin ministerium meaning occupation or office.)
2. '*I sing of a maiden*'. Anne F. Sutton. 1998 The Mercers Company. The maiden is not the Virgin Mary as the BVM, is never shown bare-breasted and does not wear a crucifix.

The worshipful Company of the Mercers (the Livery Company) was centred in London and had no country branches or country members. There were two ways of joining this rather exclusive group of merchants; by apprenticeship or by 'redemption'.[1]

Many trades-people were referred to as Mercers; by the 15th century it often meant merely 'merchant'. In Richard Whittington's time[2] the Mercers were dealing exclusively in the luxury trade in fabrics, silks, satins and cloths of gold, over which they seemed to have had a complete monopoly, but gradually they extended their range of merchandise while keeping their specialist market. They were a very strong and influential group.

Cheapside in the 1500s – home to Nicholas Ailwyn from apprentice to Lord Mayor of London.

The Mercers, with their hall in Cheapside and their neighbourhood called the Mercery, were soon vying with many other associated companies, the drapers, haberdashers, woolmen,[3] weavers, canvas makers, linen weavers and producers, tailors and hat and cap makers and sellers. Some of these became incorporated into the Mercers, some joined other companies, particularly the grocers, who took in some cloths, wool, metal and dye, and many other items other than foodstuffs. The grocers, for a time, had a monopoly in spices, while the Mercers kept their monopoly on luxury goods and added to it many other clothing and domestic commodities including wool. They were not allowed to be members of more than one company, but in 1404 John Otteley was both a Mercer and a grocer.[4]

In the 15th century there was no clear distinction between wholesale and retail; it seems many of the larger merchants were involved in both and the number of monopolies was being restricted; free competition was subject only to standards of purity in goods sold and honesty in dealing. A fairly effective system of trading standards was used by the various companies, with fines for transgressions.[5]

1. There were heavy fees for entry 'by redemption' and after 1384 it was required that a candidate had to produce six citizens of the craft to testify to his fitness and ability to pay. There were also heavy fees and sometimes a premium for apprenticeship, which was for 10 years for those over 16 years old.
2. Dick Whittington or Whyttington was Mayor in 1397, 1406, 1419.
3. 40 or 50 'woolmen' were each described as grocers and many were also members of the Staple. Merchants in Norwich were called Mercers, nearly all, which they were probably not technically.
4. The Grocers Company, mentioned first in 1180, was reorganised in 1345; 21 pepperers of Soper Lane joined canvas and rope dealers and spicers (Anevacer de Roperie and Espicer de Chepe), who were closely allied with the apothecaries and together they had formed the 'Mistery of Grossers, Pepperers and Apothecaries' by 1365. the Grossers dealt 'in gros' and by 1373 were referred to as 'Compagnie des Grossers'.
5. The Mercers controlled weights by holding the King's Beam. The Gurdler's function was to ensure that the spices were free of rubbish and impurities, and were employed by the spicers, etc.

In order to amass a sufficient fortune, Richard may have been a general merchant;[1] there was plenty of scope. Spalding was an important trading centre. He lived on the river bank but he was never identified as part of any trade. We know nothing of any warehouse or trade depot, which would have been essential for his business.

15th Century painting of merchants loading wool bags

It is very interesting to consider Robert Toppes as a contemporary Norfolk merchant, whose operation in Norwich is similar in some ways. Robert Toppes died in 1467 a very rich man, leaving a book of debts which reveal his business and transactions in great detail. Nothing like this has survived for Nicholas Ailwyn. Enough is known of Robert Toppes to say that he was a member of parliament for Norwich on six occasions and Mayor three times. Henry VII was not overly keen on calling parliaments and they were sometimes short lived. Nicholas was MP for London for one year, 1491. Both were Mercers. Robert Toppes was deeply occupied in his local business as general merchant in Norwich and did not have (as far as we know) any London interests except as an MP. Between 1468 and his death, Nicholas was concerned in national politics and was meeting kings face to face and dealing with international issues, long before he became the Warden of the Mercers in 1482. Robert Toppes does not appear to have been involved with mercers or politics.

They were both builders of note. Robert adapted an old merchant's house in Kings Street and created Toppes Hall in Norwich, now called Dragon Hall. It is a magnificent place. Robert's private house in Norwich was equally grand.

Dragon Hall (and dragon)

Nicholas built a mansion but did not have warehouses, unless they have not yet been discovered. There was insufficient storage space in his London house and only the small undercroft at Ayscoughfee, which would not have been big enough to store wool for commercial purposes.

Left: Robert Toppes in the window of St Peter Mancroft, Norwich

1. He might also have been a tanner, or involved with leather or skins.

During the 15th century, a very disturbed period for England, the raw wool market was declining, whilst the cloth trade was growing. Boston, foremost in the export of wool and wool fells to Europe through the English companies of the Staple market in Calais, was fast losing out in selling wool to be woven into cloth by the weavers of Flanders in the Netherlands.

Since Edward III, the Crown had regarded wool taxes and customs as an income, and in each reign borrowed from merchants, which sometimes amounted to forced loans. Beside the Dutch trade, English merchants were in direct competition with Merchants of the Hanse (Hanseatic League), Hansards merchants from North German towns in charge of the Baltic trade. They were privileged in England, paying lighter taxes, and English merchants, wanting to share their Baltic trade hated them and there were endless violent clashes between them.

Nicholas had to deal with problems with the 'Easterlings', merchants of the Hanse, who were particularly resented in Boston because of their privileges. They were both involved in national and local taxation at a high level, but Robert was more concerned with his constituents and he had a stronger tie with Norwich.

The fifteenth century opened with the extraordinary spectacle of the Wars of the Roses, a destructive civil war which raged during the century. The weak Lancastrian Kings could not keep order. Edward IV's usurpation and the return of Henry VI for a year. Richard III, usurper, saw the murder of the next heir to the throne and his short reign ended at the Battle of Bosworth, with a change of dynasty, heralding the first of the Tudors. Henry VII was a careful, if not parsimonious, ruler, but peace finally reigned during his time. Nicholas lived through Edward IV's reign as his first assignment was in 1468 which was a trade mission to Flanders to promote sale of English woollen cloth there.

In July 1475 and again in October 1475, he was conferring with Hugh Brice about 'customs'. Brice (or Bryce) was a goldsmith and was to be Lord Mayor in 1485, a powerful man. The subject can only be guessed at.

Nicholas' progress as a Mercer in set out in detail in the Wardens Accounts, but has to be looked at in historical context. He was also a Merchant of the Staple and may have been appointed as official representative foe the Mercers. He seems to have been given regular responsibilities in the endless negotiations. His term as Lord Mayor in 1499 was the pinnacle of his career, but long before that he moved in exalted circles. It appears he knew the Archbishop of Canterbury[1] personally and both his sons-in-law came from rich and influential aldermanic families. A close relationship with Henry Colet[2] led to land deals with Nicholas' son-in-law, Sir William Cantelowe, who played a conspicuous part in arranging high level loans and negotiating with the Exchequer in the 1450s, and he was both a Stapler and a Mercer.

But in September 1475 he assisted the Mercers' wardens to select a deputation of forty Mercers 'to ride to meet the King' (Edward IV) and to make sure his fellow Mercers were suitably dressed by buying cloth for outfits for the riders, for the meeting with the King on 22nd November.

He was to bring back the decision reached, having discussed it again with Hugh Brice. This must have been one of the many occasions when the King was demanding extra money or loans from the city, when often the Mercers came to his assistance.

In November 1479, he was chosen to 'ride to the King' about a 'subsidy', an extra sum the King demanded to be raised by the Mercers. The sum of £2000 was demanded and by January he was asked to "devise ways to please the King" as presumably they had not agreed to raise it. He could not have failed to please, for the next month he was put in charge of the arrangements for the future payment of the subsidy.

1. He gave the Archbishop a ring with a 'sleigh' on it in his will. He was William Warham Bishop of London in 1502, translated to Canterbury in 1504. They must have met during negotiations.
2. John Colet, Mercer. 1467(?)-1510, founder of St. Paul's school, son of Sir Henry. Sir Henry Colet, died in 1505 and was Lord Mayor in 1486.

Sir William Cantelowe, mercer, 'solicitor' and also Sheriff of London in 1448/49

William Cantelowe had also been described as a 'solicitor' meaning one who engages in negotiation. Nicholas seems a useful man to have about. He was called upon to assist the Wardens in all sorts of miscellaneous jobs to sort out problems over a watercourse, deliver a gift of candlesticks to the Master of St. Thomas of Acre, and to ride to meet and escort a new Mayor. On the nicer side, he attended the coronation of Elizabeth of York.

After Bosworth, Nicholas does not seem quite so active but he is soon engaged in top level discussions about the problems in Calais. Henry VII desired discussion and Nicholas was nominated to sit on the King's Council, and to represent the Mercers at a Guildhall meeting in the City of London. He then had to deliver the Mercers' answer to the Lord Treasurer in January 1486-7, and in September he was riding to the King at Warwick, to keep him informed. Tantalizingly, we do not know the outcome. In 1491 he became MP for London and an Alderman in March 1499, Master of the Mercers in 1496 and, finally, Lord Mayor of London later in 1499.

The Maidenhead was the cognisance by which members were recognised,[1] rather as coats of arms and badges were developed to identify friends or enemies on the fields of battle. The Mercers were particularly richly dressed as befitted the leading fabric company who dealt in luxuries. The luxurious wares were mainly for the female customers; skilled London silk-women made them, often merchants' wives. A woman is an appropriate logo for such a female business. The progression from badge to shop sign was obvious. In the 'Mercery' a large area from East of St. Mary le Bow, past Soper Lane, now Queen Street, was full of shops selling such delights as laces, silks, headwear, ribbons, tassels, buttons, fine kerchiefs and the more mundane blankets and coverlets. The Mercers developed into dealers exclusively for luxury goods by the time of Richard Whittington, who made a large fortune.

A later European traveller said this:

> *'Hence I passed through the Merceria which is one of the most delicious streets in the world for the sweetness of it and is all the way on both sides tapestried as it were with cloth of gold, rich damasks and other silks which the shop expose and hang before their houses from the first floor, and with that variety for near half a year spent chiefly in this city I hardly remember to have seen the same piece twice exposed. To this add the perfumer, apothecaries shops and innumerate cages of nightingales that entertain you.....'* [2]

Although written much later about a district in Italy, this passage does conjure up the wonderful sights in the Mercery[3] in London. Taverns in the area showed the brand name but whether the maiden came from a tavern sign or from some much earlier source is not known. On the edge of this area lived Nicholas Ailwyn, as he acquired a house there and would have been thoroughly familiar with the shops, lanes and alleys. He lived first in Coleman Street, in Coleman Ward, near Cheapside. The Mercery, formerly a district of Cheapside in London, where all the Mercers collected and had houses, stalls and shops, centred around Mercers Hall. The church of St. Mary le Bow,[4] was on the other side of Cheapside, which was favoured by Nicholas, but the main church connected with the Mercers was the church of St. Thomas of Acre, part of the monastery at Cheapside. The monastery church as built on a site owned by Saint Thomas á Becket's forebears, Gilbert Becket, a Norman knight who had come with his wife Roesia from Rouen, France at the time of the Conquest.

1. Sometimes the 'livery' or uniform was just a badge or particular coloured hood and sometimes it was the whole outfit. The colour seem to be varied from year to year.
2. *Evelyn's Diaries*. William Bray edition. 1818
3. Mercery is from the Latin 'merx', 'mercis', meaning wares or merchandise. The Mercery might originally have connoted all merchandise but later was silks, damasks and luxury imported goods.
4. There were 120 churches in London in the 13th century, so many for St. Mary that it was necessary to distinguish them, e.g. St. Mary Colechurch, St. Mary Aldermary, St. Mary le Bow. Le Bow was called St. Mary Arcubus, so called because of the shape of the arches.

In 1190, after Thomas' death as a martyr, Thomas and Agnes, their descendants, gave the piece of land where Thomas á Becket was born for the building of a church[1] to commemorate him. He was murdered in Canterbury in 1170. The church was St. Thomas of Acre[2] and by 1390 the Mercers were meeting there, their fraternity being recognised as patrons of the 'hospital'. Later, in 1413 they purchased a little room and chapel there, they called it Sale del Mercerie. [3]

There were twelve 'livery' companies[4] of the City of London, one for each of the main trades and they dominated City trade, holding virtual monopolies. But the Mercers considered themselves the leading company and many Lord Mayors of London were chosen from their ranks. Mercers Hall is still in Ironmonger Street and has been destroyed twice. Burned to the ground in the Great Fire of London, it was blitzed in 1941. The present building dates from 1958. The Mercers still exist as a charitable institution who support many schools[5], all founded by their members. but they are no longer involved in trade.

In 1451, at the time when Nicholas was apprenticed at about the age of fifteen, the Mercers were at the peak of their fame. His apprenticeship[6] in 1451 was with John Brodesworth, an established Mercer, and he probably lived with him and his family during his apprenticeship. By 1462 he was a 'shopholder' and able to have his own business, having completed his apprenticeship. In 1463 he blotted his copybook and was fined six shillings and eight pence for uncouth language to the Wardens, but this did not stop his progress. In 1462 he paid one shilling for the privilege of becoming a shopholder.

Life for the next twenty five years was busy; he probably went home to Spalding as often as he could, but he was active on Mercers affairs besides running his own business. His family were growing; Richard was soon followed by Joan, then another unnamed daughter and finally by Francis,[7] the youngest born between 1480-1500. His wife died before him and her name is not known.

By 1468 he was being called upon to assist in the Mercers' international diplomatic business, to speak with Customs officials, to advise on coinage and to devise rules. He was asked to help the English embassy in Flanders to enlarge their trade in woollen cloth in 1468 (probably involving a trip abroad), and by 1479 he was meeting King Edward IV about the King's money raising activities. 'To ride to the King about the subsidy' on 4th November 1479 and later that year on 29th November he was 'to ride to London at Westminster to give the Mercers answer to the King's request for a subsidy'. Early the next year, 8th January 1480, he was sent to devise 'ways to please the King about the subsidy'. It is assumed he was alone when asked to devise a 'book of complaints'[8] about foreign merchants (1480) and to reform the book of ordinances (1488) and to investigate the 'injuries' done at Calais. He seems a man of many parts.

In 1490/1 Nicholas was deputed to enquire into finding new premises for the Mercers Company. They were keen to acquire the grand Crosby Place in Bishopsgate[9] (later the home of Sir Thomas More). The same year he became MP for London and no more was heard of Crosby Place. Later the Mercers decided to enlarge their own premises.

---

1. The church of the Hospital of St. Thomas was actually 'in honour of Almighty God and the BVM and of the glorious martyr St. Thomas'.
2. Sir John Watney's account, chapter 5.
3. Ralph Agas' map of London shows the Mercers hall and chapel facing Westcheap with Ironmonger Lane on the West and the church of St. Thomas of Acre on the North. The old hall was completely destroyed in the Fire of London.
4. The name probably comes from their practice of wearing, if not an actual uniform, a hood or an identifying badge on their sleeves. Later they wore clothing of one colour for processions, but apparently varied their favoured colour.
5. St. Paul's School, Collyers College, Dauntsey's School, Abingdon School and Gresham College.
6. William Caxton was apprenticed to a Mercer in 1425 and undertook diplomatic missions for the Mercers, for Edward IV before he took up printing, publishing his first book, the Game of Chess, in 1474. He was fifteen at the time he was apprenticed, which seems the normal age, which makes Nicholas' birth 1435.
7. It is only known that Francis (Fraunceys) was under twenty one at the time of his father's death.
8. Extracts from Wardens Accounts Book 1391-1464.
9. Crosby Place has now been moved, brick by brick, to Chelsea where it has been re-erected and completely restored. It is now open to the public.

They were fortunate enough to secure, at the Reformation, the dissolved monastery[1] of Thomas of Acre and all its buildings.

In 1491 he made Richard, his oldest son, his apprentice. What happened to Richard during the next years is unknown except that he lost touch with his father and disappeared from the records. It is known that Richard had a son but he is not mentioned by name in his father's will, only his grandson, Nicholas. Either Richard died or father and son became estranged.

Nicholas had many apprentices.[2] Over the years from 1476 onwards to the time of his death he had ten and two of them survived to complete their apprenticeships after his death. Mighell English[3] and Richard Jones were both apprenticed to him. As to his business, he was probably involved in exporting wool and importing luxury goods, but before 1480 he does not feature in Boston lists of merchants or exporters.

Now at the centre of power he soon acquired rich and influential friends, knowing John Colet well. Colet was the famous founder of St. Paul's with whom he bought property. In 1491 he became an MP for London and in 1496 he moved just round the corner from Coleman Street Ward to Bassingham Ward where he was an Alderman and soon was being proposed for the office of Lord Mayor of London for the year 1499. In that year he would have entertained lavishly and expensively. He must have had many sumptuous clothes for the pageantry surrounding the office, but he does not seem to still have them by the time of his death. He leaves a fellow alderman 'my best purse of black velvet pearled with gold with double rings of silver and gilt that I wore when I was Mayor'. He did not appear to be enthusiastic about clothes or accessories, yet the priests in his two chapels were well equipped with vestments and his two houses were well furnished; and he owned a large assortment of jewellery and silver, normal for this time.

A Mercer's raison d'être; from a medieval illuminated manuscript, showing "Scenes from English Life". Bodleian library.

1. Thomas Cromwell was persuaded by Richard Gresham, a leading Mercer, to allow the Mercers to buy the whole monastery and hospital for £969.17.6 and in 1541 Henry VIII granted this by letters patent on condition they started a school, Mercers school, at their own expense.
2. Wardens Accounts Book 1391-1464
3. Mighell English became his most trusted servant, Richard Jones his attorney who Nicholas had to bale him out of trouble in 1484; no more was heard of the allegations that he was buying wares contrary to an ordinance.

CHAPTER 8

NICHOLAS' CAREER AS A MERCHANT

He does not seem to have been an ostentatious person (except in his house building). As to his business world, during the second half of the 15th century he was prosperous but it was in a climate of economic uncertainty. The export of wool was a Crown monopoly based on the exclusive wool staple market. Wool could not officially be exported after 1363 except via Calais when the Estate of Merchants formed their company there and controlled the market. Customs officials collected the revenues from customs and taxes of the wool and wool fells trade.[1] This formed the bulk of the Crown revenues, the merchants negotiating loans to the King in the hope of preferential treatment from him. Many ports exported wool, Boston was the greatest wool exporting port after London.[2] It attracted much foreign business, many Italians and Germans (Esterlings) attending the Great Fair of St. Botolph, but by the end of the 15th century the golden era of Boston port was beginning to decline, partly because the harbour had begun to silt up. Boston remained the centre for the wool trade for the surrounding wool producing counties of Lincolnshire, Leicestershire, Derby and Nottingham.

After 1363, when the wool staple was fixed in Calais, the Crown's scheme was to collect revenues directly from the port, a monopoly for the King's benefit. Wool was the wealth of England and the King's wealth too.[3] The very high tax on wool stimulated the merchants to seek an alternative, which they found in the manufacture of cloth. In Norfolk, a large weaving industry grew up around Norwich. The wool was exported from Boston to the staple clearing house in Calais. The ships returned importing all sorts of different items; first from the Hanseatic port of Lubeck[4] and Danzig. Typical cargoes were barrels of oil, firs and skins, fir board and wainscots, barrels of pitch and large quantities of stock fish (dried fish), as well as linen cloth, thread and canvas.[5]

The trade to the Netherlands was very different; ships mainly bringing in fresh fish and taking away not cloth, because Flanders was the leading cloth manufacturing centre, but manufactured goods, tiles, kettles, linen cloth and all sorts of food-stuffs, beef, bacon, wheat, barley, oats and beans. Most of the ships exporting from the port of Boston were English owned, although ships from Camfer, Schiedam, Brill and Veer brought goods from the Netherlands. There was continuous trouble with some of the foreign merchants, the Esterlings, the Hanseatic merchants from North German towns, whose presence was resented by English merchants. This is the background to Nicholas' job in 1480.

It appears that no separate customs figures have survived from Spalding, for all the ports between Wisbech and Wainfleet sent their exports to Boston where they were incorporated into Boston's returns. The Ailwyns do not appear in the names of the Boston ship-owners/masters during the years 1367-1400,[6] nor as merchants of any part of Lincolnshire during that time.

By 1486 Nicholas was involved in diplomatic work for the Mercers. He was nominated to the King's Council to discuss various questions and to present a Bill to the Lords about 'injuries' done at Calais, on behalf of the Mercers. As a spokesman for an important London company, and by 1491 also as a Member of Parliament for London, he was obviously a trusted negotiator and frequently called upon.

---

1. Wool fells are sheepskins; pellis lanuta, with the wool still on.
2. *The Trade of Boston in the Fifteenth Century* by Winifred Haward (Lincolnshire A & A Society. p.169
3. That is the reason why the Lord Chancellor sits on a woolsack, to remind the Commons that it represents the wealth of England.
4. The so-called 'Hanseatic League' kept a firm grip on the Hanseatic trade. They were given certain privileges in England which were denied to English merchants.
5. The George of Straylesund arriving in December 1463 in Boston, left with one hundred and one broad-cloths, cloth 'without grain', meaning smooth and Worsted cloth (called after the village of Worsted), was very fine and versatile and used for clothes, furnishings and even flags.
6. *Overseas Trade of Boston during the Reign of Richard II* (1367-1400). Professor Rigby.

In Norfolk a textile industry had grown up around Norwich, making Worsted cloth which was versatile and greatly in demand.[1] Edward III had encouraged Flemish textile workers and many came and settled in Norwich and by the 15th century were a well established community 'exporting' many wool workers to London who joined the Mercers. The Norwich cloth trade is relevant to the Ailwyn story because of Nicholas' involvement in 1477[2] and because of the similarities between Robert Toppes (1405-67), the mercer living in Norwich, and Nicholas Ailwyn.

The Worsted Men of Norwich (as the weavers were called) became a force to be reckoned with, as they quickly stepped in with their cloth to replace the raw wool. Their traditions of textile making and the influx of skilled workers from Flanders soon brought prosperity to Norfolk ports, Lynn and Yarmouth, at the expense of Boston. Robert Toppes[3] was a prosperous Mercer. His business book and his Will give a glimpse of his business and of his great wealth.[4]

Towards the end of the century the Boston exports dwindled, losing its trade to London, Ipswich and the new rival, Hull. The Hanseatic trade also decreased but this was partly because of the continued jealousy and friction between the Hanseatic merchants and the English, which often resulted in violence. In 1470 one Humphrey Littlebury[5] killed a German merchant in Boston. As a result the Hanseatic League withdrew their trade from Boston and excluded English ships from their ports. A redress was soon achieved but friction continued. Nicholas had to devise a book of complaints about the Esterlings in 1480, and to frame an answer to a query by Bristol Merchants in 1486.

Some of the Enrolled Customs Accounts[6] for Boston have survived for the 15th century. These were the accounts sent yearly to the Exchequer – a record of every port's traffic. The figures were entered by clerks onto rolls - long parchments six feet in length, written on both sides.

The system of customs was highly complicated, often altered and imposed heavy duties on exporters (a tax of a third of the value of the wool for English exporters). There were duties on both imports and exports, all different rates and a highly elaborate system of packing, checking and inspecting by Customs officials. There were good and bad years for wool exporters, when the wool fleet sailed in a convoy from Boston – in 1414 there were twelve ships, in 1463 only four, in 1464 eighteen and in 1465 twenty two. Later on the figures fell when the changeover from wool to cloth was complete. With an unstable government during the Wars of the Roses, this was a time when piracy and smuggling was rife and customs officials were often corrupt; a weak central government had lost control of officials.

Where the Welland runs into the sea, the Lincolnshire coast is particularly isolated and perfect for smuggling, and a great deal of illicit trade in wool went on, either by concealing wool in other commodities or by secret assignations on lonely beaches.[7] This may perhaps be one of the reasons why no figures survive for the Port of Spalding, but it seems likely that the Ailwyns may have been involved in smuggling. Tradition also has it that Spalding boats went to wait outside Boston and loaded their wares onto foreign ships on 'the Scalp' to avoid payment of customs in Boston port. Frequent cases of piracy on the high seas were reported. Boats, even in fleets, left Boston only to be captured outside the mouth of the Witham and their cargoes sold elsewhere. French pirates attacked ships and sold their cargoes in Cromer. Many examples of this appear in the Customs Accounts.[8]

---

1. *The Linen and Worsted Industry of Norfolk.* Anne F. Sutton. Norfolk and Norwich Archaeological Society. 1989, p201
2. In August 1477 Nicholas was 'devising' a bill 'against the Worsted Men of Norwich' and 'persons going to Calais'. At the moment there is no explanation of the meaning of this note.
3. *The Life and Times of a late Medieval Norwich Merchant.* Christopher Barringer and Neil Sigsworth (Norfolk and Norwich Heritage Trust 2002)
4. The 'Great Book'. Norfolk Record Office. DCN 9/5.
5. Humphrey Littlebury of Kirton was a Customs Officer in Boston and he may be related to the Humphrey Littlebury of the grand tomb in Holbeach Parish Church who died in about 1400.
6. LTR Enrolled Accounts (Customs) (See Winifred Haward)
7. *The Trade of Boston in the Fifteenth Century* by Winifred I. Harward.
8. National Archives (customs accounts).

As Nicholas would know well of these perils, it may be that he avoided Spalding and Boston and conveyed his wares to London for exporting abroad.[1] In 1480 he is recorded as exporting from London[2] wool and cloth in the ships of Thomas Coys of London (one bale with fourteen cloths, one bale with two cloths), and in 1481 he is again mentioned as exporting (one bale with fourteen cloths) from London.

To investigate the suggestion that the Ailwyns were smuggling we have to go back to Richard.[3] The organisation called the Staple (or Fellowship) consisted solely of merchants who were involved in exporting wool. Unfortunately, no complete list exists for the relevant time but it is known there were about 300 Staplers in all. Richard is generally described as a Stapler.

A 1536 picture of splendid Russian envoys and merchants from the Baltic, ready to sell their furs to foreign merchants.

The Staplers customs system was extremely complicated and taxes had to be paid upon leaving England through the customs at the ports.[4] All wool had to go to the mart in Calais which had a monopoly of selling wool. More taxes were payable before it was distributed by purchasers mainly from Holland, Zealand and Italy. Prices were fixed by the Staple.

The English wool growing areas produced 51 varieties of kinds of wool. March and Cotswolds were the most prized (12 marks), but in Lincolnshire, Lindsey, Newark and North Holland were also considered good (7½ marks). Kesteven and South Holland came next (7 marks), while the wool from Kent, Suffolk and Sussex was poor and sold for 2 marks.

Richard Ailwyn was almost certainly dealing in raw wool. Whether he was involved in collecting farmers' wool from a 'brogger'[5] or exporting it, or both, or was involved in some other process, cannot be deduced. His name does not appear in the extensive Boston records, nor does it for Lynn or Wisbech for the relevant time, the end of the 14th century to the middle of the 15th century. Whatever he was engaged in, by 1450 he was in a position to think about and make grandiose plans for a proposed building. Perhaps he already lived on the site and pulled down what was there; no excavation under ground on either Ayscoughfee or Gayton has ever been undertaken, so there is no way of knowing. He had sufficient capital in hand to embark on this project.

1. The merchant exporters always split their loads between ships to minimise their losses and sailed in a fleet of ships for protection.
2. Petty Custom Account 1480-1. Exports (484-520)
3. *Studies in English Trade in the 15th Century*. Eileen Power and M. Postan. 2nd Edition. 1951.
4. The designated wool ports were, in order of importance, London, Boston, Ipswich, Hull and occasionally Lynn, Poole, and Chichester.
5. A Brogger is a broker, a middle-man, also called a woolman or a woolmonger.

A scene of a busy continental market place, probably Antwerp, in the 15th century

His portrayal in the Roundel shows a jolly, smiling face but perhaps he looks a bit of a ruffian. If the child is Richard junior, it may date from about 1476. Richard has a long beard, a fashionable hat and natty little boots, with a walking stick or wand of office held in his hands, and he looks full of vigour, contentment and prosperity.

The smuggling of raw wool[1] for the export trade was rife in his lifetime but participation in this would explain why his name never appears in any official list of ship owners or exporters, nor is he described in any official capacity. With one exception. There is an undated document,[2] addressed to 'the King' when 'Richard Ailwyn' and another man are requested to produce documents in the Court of Chancery by Henry of Cambridge, Bailiff of Billingsgate relating to several ports, Sluis, Gravesend, Billingsgate, London River and their 'customers'.[3] Although slim evidence, with no information about the sequel, it is some evidence that old Richard might have made his money smuggling, but this time he was caught.

1. Wool was smuggled because of the very heavy duty on it; it was concealed with other wares and there are hundreds of cases of people caught in the Thames Estuary, Southampton and Lincolnshire. And there was corruption in the customs. See Haward.
2. The document is a 'cocket', a term for a docket, a kind of receipt to show customs duty has been paid. The document is probably 14th century but not dated. Special Collections (Ancient Petitions) 4451-4500.
3. 'Customers' are Customs officials.

CHAPTER 9

NICHOLAS' WILL

Nicholas' will is a document of marathon proportions. Dictated to his scrivener by Nicholas on 2nd October 1503, it runs to over eight closely written pages, with detailed and meticulous directions for his funeral[1] and *Month's Mind*, hundreds of small bequests and legacies to his household, his business colleagues and his family. William Carkeke, his scrivener, was well rewarded for his pains by a handsome legacy, £26.13.4d as an expression of "the special love that I owe him". As everyone else at this time, Nicholas was concerned above all for his soul, and those of his family, and wished to ensure them a good reception in Heaven. Nicholas believed that saying masses for his soul after his death and paying for them, even reading his name out during church services,[2] would achieve this. During his life-time he might have tried to perform the five corporal works of mercy, to visit the sick, visit the imprisoned, clothe the naked, feed the hungry, house the homeless and to comfort the afflicted, and his will reflects his desire to continue these duties after his death. He was probably not overly religious but religion was then a much more central part of life and he was clearly a regular and well informed church goer, and generous in his benefactions during his lifetime. Surprisingly, he did not give away great sums for grandiose charitable foundations, schools or monasteries, and the Mercers were not beneficiaries. He leaves them jewels to the value of £13.6.8d, but many of them were remembered by name in his will. He also donates a sum for a tapestry "a hankyng of tapestry to serve for the high dees in the guylde hall."

His "great place[3] in Spalding" is left to his youngest son Francis (Fraunceys), still under twenty-one. His eldest son and heir Richard is not referred to except as "the father of Nicholas" who will inherit everything if Francis does not survive to 26 years. All his real property is left in the same way. Elaborate precautions are set up to protect the estate during the boy's minorities. Provision for upkeep, a housekeeper and everything to be left as it is, until one of the boys can take possession. Both are young, Nicholas about 11 and Francis probably about the same.

His original family is sadly depleted by the time of his death. His unnamed wife is dead, so are his two daughters. Richard, who was his eldest son, must also be dead; he may not have lived after completing his apprenticeship, although he was still alive in 1492 and described as Mercer. The carving of the young mercer apprentice in the Spalding Parish Church may well be the only memorial to Richard. Nicholas' "late wife" is to be prayed for twenty years in St. Mary le Bow, but she has no memorial and no masses. Richard himself is not mentioned at all.

Nicholas is equally economical with his two daughters. Joan is simply referred to as 'my daughter called Cantelowe', perhaps he has forgotten her name. Joan made a very good marriage to Henry Cantelowe, the son of Sir William Cantelowe, Mercer and Alderman of the City of London. Her burial place he remembers as Streatham, where she has a tomb. His bequest to the church wardens ensures that her tomb should be lit by five tapers every Easter 'until the money runs out'. When she died is not known, but he is clearly familiar with the church for he also gives money for its repair in his will.

It is said Henry Cantelowe died in 1490. Joan and Henry had a daughter, another Joan, who survived to marry Oliver Wode, later both seem to be part of Nicholas' household. Being his granddaughter she was also given the only book that Nicholas possessed. This was described as a *'Prymer [4] written in Pchemyn with two silver elapses (clasps?) corded with blake damask'*.

---

1. A commemoration mass and service on the first monthly anniversary after the death.
2. Bederoll, Beadroll. A list of names to read out during the service and to be prayed for.
3. Ayscoughfee Hall.
4. This may be a prayer book, or book to teach children to read (Primer). Pchemyn may connote a book of engraved plates or wood cuts, or may merely mean parchment. He was obviously not a reading man. John Paston, the merchant from Norfolk in the same century, had a large quantity of books on all sorts of subjects, only one printed, the rest in manuscript.

The daughter of Oliver received *'an Agnus Dei of Gold Wit a Ruby and II Orient Pies Wit Spangles Pendant,.*[1] while Richard Cantelowe, his grandson, got a *'ring of gold brayded or wreathed'* while Richard's wife got a *'ring of base gold'*.

The two main beneficiaries received remembrances; Nicholas *'my ring of gold with a Thakes –'* (head is perhaps the word omitted), while Frances a *'great hoop of base gold set with a diamond and a ruby that I was wont to wear'*. In the middle of the family list comes the gift of a *'fine gold signet with the symilitude of a sleigh (sledge) there on'* to the Archbishop of Canterbury, a strange gift for him.

His other unnamed daughter married a draper called William Heriott or Heryot.[2] Her child, is referred to obliquely as "the daughter of William Heriott, my son-in-law". She is given £6.13.4d but her name is not revealed, nor is her mother's.

Nicholas appoints two executors.

Mighell English - £100 legacy, his wife given "a great hooped ring of fyn gold".

Angel Donne - £40 legacy and a gold sovereign.

He then names his six house servants and gives them their sums of money. His chamberlain, William Millborne and his wife (who is also a cornemeter is forgiven his debt for £3.6.8d) heads another list including Alice Hedges' son William Hoffey and other servants of his household. Alice, his housekeeper, is given furs, £50, his low bed, some furniture and silver.

He then appoints five overseers (supervisors) of his will who get £10 each.

William Parer (Gentleman)
Richard Bertes (mercer)
Hugh Smith (servant, mercer)
John Ashe (wax chandler)
Nicholas Tickhill (mercer, servant)

This gives a final figure of about thirteen people. It can be fairly safely assumed that Nicholas died at his house in the churchyard of St. Mary le Bow. A glimpse of it and the contents "of the house where I dwelt" appear in his will. It does not seem to us a very comfortable or luxurious house, containing a hall, parlour, buttery, great chamber, chapel, kitchen and several bed chambers, office, a small yard and stable.

Following the usual plan, in the hall was a long table on the raised dais for the family, servants and guests, with one chair and seven joint stools. In the body of the hall were four trestles, two side tables and benches and forms, enough to seat a lot of people. As he employed at least fifteen people and may have kept open house, they would have been needed. In his private chapel, an alabaster altar and desks. In the parlour were many more tables, trestles and stools. In the buttery, there were shelves and "almey bins" for storing things. The counting room with shelves and cupboards. The great chamber (his bedroom) had a free standing bed with "bordes" and a long table, trestles, a cupboard. It is the house of a working merchant with no sign of a female presence. No mention of the usual comforts of hanging tapestries or floor coverings.

In the kitchen only one brush. In the yard, two brushes or brooms, there is a coop for chickens in the stable but no horse. Perhaps these are just the basics that he wanted leaving. All these items are not willed but left in place. He makes the same provision for his house in Spalding.

---

1. This was probably a miniature or figure of a golden lamb bearing a cross with pearls of the orient for eyes (pies may be a misprint), meaning of spangles has not changed.
2. William Heriott had a memorial in Spalding church, now disappeared. *'Orate pro aia Willi Heriot Militis Mercatoris Stapule Calisiae Et Parm Civitas London'. An Account of the Churches of South Holland*, published from Holles 1843. A coat of arms was nearby. 'A fesse engrailed between 3 lions rampant'. The Ailwyn coat.

Nicholas sets out his plans to help those imprisoned. He even leaves a sum of £20 to "secure prisoners' release", specifying Ludgate Prison and the old Newgate Prison (shown left), limited to 13s/4d for each prisoner. £40 is to be spent on ha'penny bread for the poor prisoners in Ludgate, Newgate, the two Compters, the Kings Bench, the Marshalsea, the Fleet, the Gatehouse and the convict prison at Westminster.[1]

Alice Hedge is to organise this distribution and to take one penny in the shilling for her reward and to hand out one of his half-penny loaves "when need shall be". As she is also asked to be the custodian of his house in Spalding "if she will", she cannot be in two places at once, but it is not known which she chose.

His bequests to Spalding were fairly divided between the Parish Church (a vestment of red worsted from his London chapel) and to the Priory a white one to the altar of the Lady of the North Door.[2] He gave money for the repair of the cloister of the Priory, and to the Parish Church the most important item was "To the full gilding and garnishing of the rood loft in the Parish Church of Spalding or other things after discretion of my executors".[3] Three of the Guilds of Spalding and Cowbit received varying sums[4] and the parish clerks of Spalding got £2.6.8d between them.

His will spreads his beneficence to Spalding, Cowbit, Moulton and Pinchbeck. Roads are to be repaired, particularly the road from London to Spalding and Spalding to Pinchbeck. Friends are remembered in the villages. Roads as far away as Bridgewater, Dunstable, Streatham, Croydon are specified and Peterborough bridge. Also the bridge that he made during his lifetime "through the park towards Pinchbeck" all get £3.6.8d. (There are two bridges in Pinchbeck that he had made.)

Cowbit Church in 1820 – Watercolour by Hilkiah Burgess, from the Spalding Gentlemen's Society collection

The chapel in Cowbit is to receive £10 and he desires prayers for him to be said there for twenty years. He gives the vicar of Pinchbeck 20d. and to six priests 12d each for them to say a mass and requiem for him. At Weston, a requiem mass is to be said for which he pays the vicar 20d and 4 priests each to be paid 12d. As to the poor, nine poor men and women of Cowbit and Peakhill are to be paid 10d for praying for his soul and those of his family. The Pinchbeck poor and the poor of Moulton are given 4d each and so are the poor of Weston. Only the poor of Cowbit have to perform a service of prayer in return.

1. The Fleet and the Compters were debtors' prisons and the Gatehouse was a prison over the gate of the palace of Westminster.
2. Our Lady of the North Door, must be a reference to a special altar in the church near the market place.
3. Whether he or his father Richard gave this screen is not known but it can still be seen in the south porch of Spalding Parish Church. It does not appear ever to have been gilded but it has been sadly battered by the elements since it has stood outside in the open porch.
4. Trinity Guild £3.6.8d, St. John's Guild 40/-, Trinity Guild of Cowbit 20/-.

He names his friends in Moulton, Harrison and his wife, and the vicar of Pinchbeck (John Toofte[1] or Toft), the widow Ayleward of Weston and many other names. The vicar also gets the option of a black funeral outfit and seventeen other people, including Master Ogle and the Harrisons of Moulton, are also offered the outfit. Some got clothes; Oliver Wode is given "my symsyn gown lined with damask and three yards of velvet". John Mosse, his valet (mentioned elsewhere) gets "the bedding he lies on" and free accommodation for the next ten years as well as forty shillings. Nicholas Tykhill and Hugh Smith share the "featherbed, the bolster, blankets and the coverlet that they now use to lie on", so they are still with him as his personal servants.

Five godsons (all called Nicholas) all get 6/8d, one goddaughter (he cannot remember her name) got 20/-. Small sums go to eight named people and to 'Margaret with one hand'. She is right at the end of the list; he is obviously observant and was touched by this poor lady and remembered her. There follows bequests to Master and monks of St. Thomas of Acre and many other convents, sums for St. Mary's, Saint Bartholomew's, St. Thomas' hospitals and the "poor people of St. Giles"[2] and to eight convents with separate sums for the lady prioresses. A great many tradesmen are given legacies. He does not forget his notary Richard Jones, who has apparently been forgiven for getting him into trouble in 1484.

There follows an assortment of good causes, relieving poor prisoners, helping poor householders, paying maintenance for boys at university, marrying poor maidens and £40 towards repairs to "Noyous weyes and bridges". A sum for £20 of vestments to be given to poor churches. All of his twelve apprentices, John Fayre, Hugh Smith, Robert Smith and William Talys get £10, but John Fayre gets only £6.13.4d because Nicholas remembers the £14.0.7d "he owes to me by my reckoning" – so long ago!

At his death he lived in his 'great house' in the churchyard of St. Mary le Bow; this house would have been sufficiently grand for the residence of a Lord Mayor of London. This house remained in the family until his son Francis and Bridget, his wife, lived in it after his death. Francis inherited this house but its final fate is still unknown.

Nicholas appears to have owned properties both in London and in Lincolnshire . He had some land in Spalding near the vicarage and it is said he had property in Pinchbeck, Gosberton and Stamford. In Cordwainer Street in the parish of Bow, he had 'four messuages', inherited by Francis[3] who sold off three of them. In Lincolnshire, he bought, with others, 300 acres and ten houses in Marston. With the Coler family he bought a share in the manor of Chipsby in Norfolk. It is said he owned property in Southwark and had several houses in London, in Soper Lane, St. Martin Pomeroy and St. Mary le Bow.

In 1492 a transaction is recorded; Nicholas bought Clements Inn in London. Richard Ailwyn (described as a Mercer) shared equally in the purchase. It was for the use of Henry Cantelowe, Mercer. This Inn was one of the ancient inns of Chancery and was not a public house, but a college of law. To find what the purchase was intended for would require a great deal of research. It is interesting because it is the last mention of Richard, who is there described as a Mercer and Henry Cantelowe is said to have died in 1490. In 1892 the Mercers purchased another old inn, Barnards Inn, to use for their school. What use Henry Cantelowe was to put it to requires much enquiry.

All his personal belongings are given by will and later codicils. His valuable sadlery is reserved for his London friends. Perhaps the oddest thing is that he does not appear to have cash in hand or to be selling anything. He has business assets but they are all in Calais; he is obviously still trading right to the end. The wool consists of raw wool and skins with wool left on (wool fells), some old and some new. None of the dozens of bequests are to be paid until the proceeds of sale of his wool are in the hands of the executors, with one exception, William Carkeke should be paid his £26.13.4d.

---

1. John Toofte, to whom there is no reference in the Pinchbeck Register.
2. A leper hospital.
3. It appears Francis was a wastrel and got into serious debt. Francis let the house out to provide income for himself. By 1518 he was in debt and he was not heard of after 1520.

All the rest of his goods and chattels and debts are left to Francis and Nicholas, to be kept for them until they are 26 years. If they both die, the sums accrued shall be divided in five parts, for poor prisoners for marrying poor maidens and poor householders. It may have been a large sum.

His Aldermanic friends are remembered. Roger Acheley is given a horse halter complete, and "my best purse of black velvet pearled with gold with double rings of silver and gilt that I wore when I was Mayor." John Warner gets a "saddle of light tawny velvet and the harness with gilt bolyons".[1]

Medieval purse, as found in the stained glass at Tattershall Castle.

His gifts to roads and churches demonstrate how much he travelled and observed. He noticed the Parish Church of St. Mary Stanning, St. Mary's in Milk Street, Streatham, the steeple of St. Mary le Bow, St. Thomas of Acre, St. Margaret's.[2] All needed repair. He specifies that they take down the north side of St. Margaret's church to "make the street wider" (£6.13.4d). He noticed that the Wyke in Dover (sea defences and a landing place) needed repair and left money for that. Perhaps he remembered uncomfortable nights in Dover and so left a fund for bedding at Maison Dieu, Dover.

Nicholas has two favourites; his housekeeper, Alice Hedge and his ex-apprentice, Mighell English, whom he particularly valued. Alice Hedge is preferred above other female servants and is given £50 and treated most generously. She is given a fine ring with a ruby and pointed diamond, a cupboard with an aumbry, "a remyngtalle therein",[3] his own low bed "that I am wont to be on with the canopy and the coverlet of tapestry with the three Kings of Cologne[4] with all other things belonging to the same", and a goblet of silver and hanging beam in his chamber with five candlesticks, a silver salt and three silver spoons.[5]

Mighell English is his most trusted servant and is given £100, and is described as "my faithful, trust servant whom I have ever found fine to the same extent". Two more servants, Robert Smith and William Tales should be "made free of the staple of Calais at my expense."

A great deal of thought has gone into this comprehensive will. Perhaps he had been ill for some time (the low bed) and had plenty of time to think over the contents. He emerges as a kindly and generous man whose lapses of memory over the names of his children and grandchildren could be explained in other ways than mere loss of memory that comes with age. Nicholas died in London and in his will requests to be buried "in the north side of the quire under the sepulchre that John Worship did make". Although unnamed, this church must be St. Mary le Bow[6] of Cheapside. He arranges for a sum to be allowed for 'works' to the chancel and for repairs generally for the church. He also allows £20 extra for a "tombe of marbille"[7] to be set "over my grave" at his executors' discretion. His sepulchre was planned well in advance and was already in place.

1. Bolus, a gilt nob.
2. In his will, Robert Toppes of Norwich left money to every church in Norwich, over 50 of them.
3. It is unclear what a remyngtalle is.
4. The Magi, a popular design at this time.
5. The weight of all this silver is given as 22oz.
6. Maria de Arcubus. This 11th century church was so called because it was built with an arched crypt and was the place of meeting of the Court of Arches. Part of the steeple fell down in 1271, the church was destroyed in the Great Fire and rebuilt by Wren. *Old London City Churches* (London Society), price 1/-.
7. It will never be known whether his 'tombe of marbille' was erected as the whole church was burnt to the ground in the Fire of London.

Meticulous arrangements were made for this grand London funeral, four priests and four men in the Mercers' livery, each one to be paid. His personal named wax chandler was to make a "robust herse" [1] and provide candles. The poor men holding the torches were to be paid and each given a black livery gown and hood. He orders that the priest officiating should be Dr. Fawderby[2] and specifies that an "honest priest of good conversation and virtuous disposition be employed to sing for my soul".

Nicholas was clearly frugal but anxious to create a spectacle and the torches, candles and tapers were an expensive commodity; as he was knowledgeable about wax he did not want any waste. His wax chandler, obviously a close friend, John Ashe, was mentioned in the will several times. He was to make two dozen torches for both ceremonies and for the procession, given £6.13.4d (10 marks) to spend on the wax, and he is to make an 'honest herse' which in those days meant a metal holder for candles. He should be paid £6.13.4d including the wax. The workmanship for a 20lb candle would be very large and wasteful[3] and John Ashe is to be present during the time they are lit and paid for his attendance to ensure they are lit and extinguished by the sexton. Two smaller candles, 4lbs each, should burn during services. An elaborate list is set out for the disposal of the 14 torches, weighing 20lbs, which he requires for Spalding ceremonies.[4]

Funeral mass from a breviary on vellum. French, circa 1340.

A list of people who should be given enough black cloth for a funeral gown follows; this cloth should be "suitable for their degree" and chosen by his executors. His two executors, Mighell English and his wife, Angel Donne and his wife, his main household servants, his chamberlain, his attorney, his two main beneficiaries, his scrivener, his notary and his wax chandler, and forty five other named people are listed to be clothed. More of his Spalding mourners who will attend are given black gowns. Fourteen local people are led by Mistress Gayton[5] and John Toofte, the vicar of Pinchbeck, all of whom are given small bequests. Some are old friends from Moulton and Weston, despite his years away from Spalding.

Dramatically, he leaves three thousand pounds to poor people within the liberties of London – 12d each and has worked out it would cost £150. This presumably would be distributed at the funeral.

1. A herse or hearse.
2. Dr. Fawderby or Fotherby, Rector of St. Peter's, Cornhill, also gets a pair of beads of coral with ten aves, a rosary.
3. In the Paston Letters, there is a complaint that 20/- spent on wax at a funeral was excessive.
4. The parishioners of Moulton were threatened with excommunication by the Bishop of Lincoln if they helped themselves to the candles round the bier after the funeral.
5. This is the only mention of a 'mistress Gayton', perhaps the 'next door neighbour', the mistress may connote an older lady and she heads the list – could she be his mother-in-law?

The funeral procession[1] would have been very impressive; robed priests, mercers in their coloured livery 'bearing his body to the sepulchre'. The night before a service would be held in the church where his body lay[2].

After the funeral, the twenty-four torches were to be set at his burial. The coffin was to be followed by twenty-four poor men, each of whom would be dressed in gowns and hoods of black linen and paid. For the next twenty years on the anniversary, a service should be held with prayers for the souls of Nicholas, "my late wife and my children" and he set aside a large sum for services for priests' wages, bills, bread, ale, wine, spices and a cash distribution amongst the poor. Some refreshments were provided and the sum calculated. Daily for a month after his death, he wanted ten priests and two clerks to say a mass of requiem 'by rote' at St. Mary le Bow. Then he requested that six thousand poor people should be given a penny, to be distributed amongst them, the poor of London, which he calculated at £25.

The candles and torches used he specified all to local altars in Spalding and Cowbit. Obviously, he trusts John Ashe for he expresses no such worry about his London funeral. One month after his death his Months Mind service was to be held in London at St. Mary le Bow, then 'with all goodly haste' a Months Mind service must also take place at Spalding.

So, the scene moves to Spalding. He has arranged every detail and thought of everything. The two services of his months mind commemoration are to be held simultaneously at the Parish Church and the conventual church. A contingent of his mourners are to travel to Spalding in advance. His two executors, his five supervisors, close friends, a cook, sixteen men and one woman (Alice Hedge) are to 'find horses' and he will pay all their expenses for meat, drink and 'horsemeat'.[3] In advance, he orders the bells to be rung and a bellman to go round the town, telling the townspeople to pray for his soul.[4] Twelve priests, four parish clerks, the sexton, all attending, are to be paid 8d and twelve children are to attend in surplices and receive 4d each. Nicholas wants a smart turn-out and a day Spalding town will remember. His sixteen mourners are each to have three yards for a black gown. Forty poor men of Spalding and Cowbit are also provided with gowns of northern tawney,[5] each gown to cost four shillings.

To make it all memorable, he wills that three thousand people within Spalding and Cowbit 'men, women and children, servants, rich and poor' should be given 12d each. As to Spalding Priory, and the servants there, he gives 6/8 to each of twenty-four monks, money for the ringers, the clerks, the prior as well as twelve other local priests and the sexton.

His mourners for this service are his local friends, relations and family. They are all to have a black gown at his expense. The list is headed by Mistress Gayton and there are eighteen others featured, most of whom have been already given legacies.

To keep his memory fresh, his name is to be read out every Sunday from the pulpit, as part of the Bederoll for twenty years, praying for him, his father and mother and all Christian souls, and 'Squire Garton'. And for the next twenty years, a rather touching ceremony will take place every Sunday in Spalding church.

---

1. The procession did not have far to go, just round the corner, in fact.
2. Henry VII, who died in 1509, was planning his funeral and tomb for many years in advance. He wanted 10,000 masses for his soul and planned the magnificent chapel in Westminster Abbey for his resting place.
3. Feed for the horses.
4. Apparently, this custom is peculiar to Spalding.
5. Northern tawney is brown cloth.

He describes it all in detail:

"An honest priest of good conversation wearing his surplice, should come to the gravestone of my father and mother between Matins and Mass, having collected twenty-eight poor men and women with him and to stand there and recite the Psalm de Profundis Clamari."[1] If they 'cannot say it' they should recite one paternoster, one ave, one credo for "*Richard Ailwyn, Margaret, his wife, and of me, Nicholas Ailwyn, their son Robert Gayton*" and for 'all Christian souls'. *"One of the poor men should repeat this aloud, and all the others shall say 'Amen'. Each of the twenty-eight poor men should receive 1d every Sunday and the priest's pay is calculated for twenty years."*

The people of Spalding must have found this a great day, and would have remembered it, although Nicholas Ailwyn's name has now passed into obscurity.

Scenes from a funeral in French Book of Hours circa 1475
The main picture shows the coffin being brought to church,
while the bottom picture shows Lazarus, rising from the dead.

1. The punctuation is not helpful. 'Out of the depths I cry to you, oh Lord' psalm 130.

CHAPTER 10

BISHOP RUSSELL AND THE AILWYNS

Bishop Russell of Lincoln (1480-1494) may have known the Ailwyn family. They also must have known the Prior of Spalding, Thomas of Moulton IV,[1] who was a particular friend of the Bishop.

Bishop Russell[2] was above all a statesman and administrator and was an absentee bishop for sometime, spending little time in his large diocese, being very much involved in state business, first for Edward IV as negotiator and later Chancellor of England. After Bosworth, when the country settled down with the first Tudor, Henry VII, he also undertook royal negotiations, but then spent much more of his time in Lincolnshire and his diocese. He acted as peacemaker between the battling monasteries in Lincolnshire who continually quarrelled with each other, particularly Spalding and Crowland.

The arms of Bishop Russell on the Inner Gatehouse at Buckden Towers (1480) near Huntingdon, home to the Bishops of Lincoln.

Tradition has it that Bishop Russell consecrated the chapel at Ayscoughfee in 1486, while a guest of the Ailwyn family.[3] This story seems to have been accepted without question but there is no evidence to support it. He claims the chapel was in the room later used as the billiard room. There is more than a suggestion of a small oratory over the porch, which still exists, but if there was a chapel,[4] its site has not yet been established.[5]

In 1868 when the house was sold, the sales description describes two billiard rooms on the ground floor. So far no-one has any information about which rooms they were. However, the east room on the first floor has been recently designated as the chapel and although there is no reason why it should not be 'upstairs',[6] as it would be a private chapel for only the family and staff. An oratory for private prayer near the downstairs entrance, which could be used by visitors, could be in addition or instead of a chapel. Nicholas certainly had his own chapel in his London house where mass was celebrated. His chapel was furnished with an alabaster altar and desks. In his will, Nicholas leaves to the altar of St. John[7] in the Parish Church of Spalding, the vestments of "rede worstead that my chapleyn wears when he doth syng at the altar of my house, with all things that longeth thereto". But there is no mention of any resident chaplain at Ayscoughfee.

The East room has no notable features, except a fireplace. This may be very ancient and has not been fully excavated but its site could not have been altered; it is built into the north wall, partly covered by a much later 18th century stone fireplace with a 19th century over mantel. This fire would have provided warmth for the congregation's backs and the altar would have been at the other end. It would have made an odd chapel and it is difficult to imagine it as a billiard room.

1. Prior Thomas IV. There is some uncertainty about the tenure of this prior, who Maurice Johnson claims was one of the de Multones of Moulton, whose memorial in a window of the Moulton Parish Church was destroyed. Gooch claims he was prior for 22 years but this is not confirmed by other sources. He was also the owner of the seal found at Cherry Willingham, now in the author's possession.
2. DNB. Bishop John Russell, died 1494. Lincs. Arch. Episcopal Register 22.
3. E. H. Gooch. P17.
4. HBA paragraph 3.3 p34.
5. In 1307 there were two licensed private chapels recorded in Spalding, belonging to Richard de Hoddell and Joseph Hare, according to Mr. Maratt, but he gives no source for this information.
6. Woodcraft Castle of civil war fame, a much earlier building, has an upstairs domestic chapel with a fireplace and separate stairway.
7. An alabaster altar would have been a small stone table. Alabaster is semi transparent gypsum, produced in Leicestershire and Nottingham, then very popular for church carvings.

The East Room in 2005, showing the original fireplace partially concealed by a later stone example from around 1700. Also note the exposed timbers above.

The puzzling piece of stonework at the side of the fireplace can be interpreted in several ways. It is a square headed niche with a stone lintel which contains a stone basin and a small drain hole in one of its corners.[1]

It has been suggested it is a stoup for holy water, but water that has been blessed to dip your fingers in would not have a hole for draining and as any good Catholic knows, your left hand is not used and holy water has to be carefully disposed of and not into a sewer. Stoups are usually on the right, near a door. It seems to be in the wrong place to be a receptacle for washing holy mass vessels, (a laver or piscina) and is far too small. Usually this is a round basin set in or against the wall, south of the altar and has a drain.

It looks 'built in', it does not conclusively prove the room's use. Dr. Jonathan Clark thinks it may well be either a stoup or a laver. However, I believe it is much more likely to have been a receptacle for salt, near the fire to keep it from getting damp.[2]

Permission had to be sought to have a private chapel usually in the care of a stipendiary clerk who was not expected to undertake other pastoral duties if the chaplain lived in. No such permission can be traced. Locally, there were not many. Lawrence Holbeach had one at his house in Holbeach in 1300[3] and Clement Hatfield was granted permission at Wykham in 1311.

As to the assertion about the 'consecration' of the Ayscoughfee chapel in 1486, it is known that Bishop Russell was in the vicinity in April 1486. He stayed at Crowland Abbey, on a peace-making mission.

1. p34. para. 3.3.3 HBA (Historic Buildings Assessment) January 2006.
2. There is a similar receptacle at Rockingham Castle, by the side of a vast 'open' fireplace in the great hall. A fireplace upstairs would be a good place to keep salt safely and free from damp, as it was a valuable commodity.
3. Margaret Paston (the Paston Letters vol. 2, p152) in 1474 asked the Bishop of Norwich for permission to have their own chapel because she was 'too sickly to go outside to church'. She was aggrieved because she sought a lifetime's permission but only got one month. There are many records for fines imposed for having an unlicensed chapel. There is evidence of two private chapels in Spalding. (See Maratt)

He settled a dispute in Stamford over an almshouse; he redrafted statutes of Leicester's Newark College and made peace between Crowland and Peterborough Abbeys, and almost certainly consecrated a chapel in Cowbit, now the Parish Church.[1]

Cowbit and the Parish Church there was favoured by the Ailwyns,[2] who remembered many in Nicholas' will. It has an interesting history.[3] Cowbit was an ancient Chantry belonging to Spalding Priory who provided a priest, although it was only five miles from Crowland. Cowbit and Pikale (now Peakhill) were far flung hamlets, deep in the Fens and quite cut off in bad weather. In 1363, a parochial chapel existed but by 1396 it was ruined and unusable. The villagers set to and built themselves another chapel, helped no doubt by their benefactors. Thomas of Moulton, the then Prior of Spalding, joined with the Ailwyn family and by 1486 it was completed, with bells and windows in place. Some of thc ancient chantry material was re-used. The corbel heads are ancient and so is the carved fish on the outside wall.

The Bishop was a particular friend of Thomas of Moulton and he was persuaded to consecrate the rebuilt chapel. On 11th May 1486 the Bishop visited Cowbit and conferred the rites of sacrament and burial and later confirmed it with his Episcopal seal. The parishioners were to maintain it and to hire a 'fit and able priest'[4] and the Prior of Spalding consented to this arrangement, while the parishioners agreed to pay one quarter of 'church assessments' to Spalding.

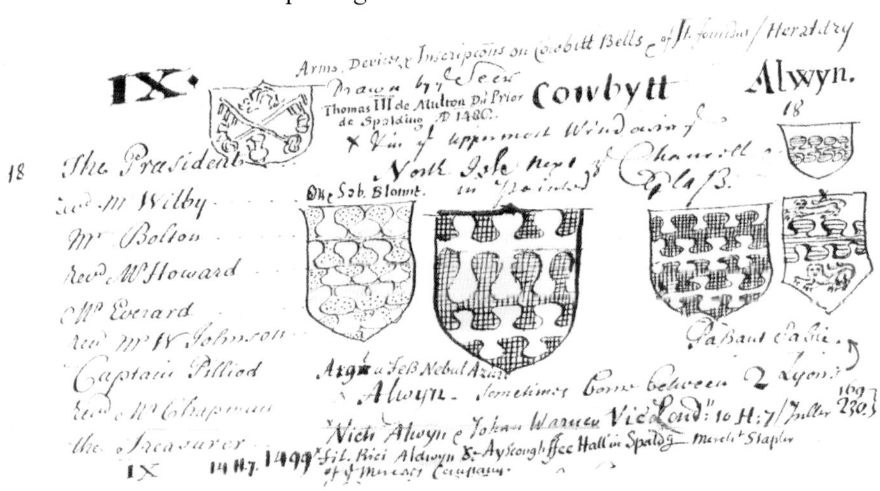

The Ailwyns contributed money, but their main gift were the bells. They were engraved with the Ailwyn coat of arms, and Maurice Johnson noted them in his minutes for 1724. (left) It has not been possible to cxamine the present bells in Cowbit tower.[5] As benefactors, their coat of arms was put into the stained glass windows 'over the altar'.[6]

Unfortunately, they do not seem to have survived. Two of the bells were examined by Mr. Maratt in the 19th century and he did not understand the 'devices' saying:

'Whether these devices are enigmatical, or whether they are figures of things they are meant to represent is too difficult to find out..... The wheat sheaf is no enigmatic ingenuity it being the arms of the priory'.[7]

He goes on to point out all the spelling mistakes of the 'monkish inscriptions' on the two other bells. So it appears that the Bishop's visit to Ayscoughfee may be pure conjecture by Gooch.

---

1. Medieval Chapels in Lincoln. Dorothy Owen. LHA vol. 10
2. Nicholas left to 'poor men and women of Cowbit (Spalding) a gown of northern tawney, each gown containing 3 verges of broad cloth' to the chapel of Cowbit some torches and some money, and a sum of money to MMM men, women and children 'riche and poure within Spalding and Cowbit' and a sum to the Cowbit Trinity Guild.
3. Cowbit church is shown thatched in a Burgess watercolour of 1818. It was on the shore of Cowbit wash, a large inland lake, where fishermen are drying their nets on the shore.
4. In 1631 an inspeximus (confirmation) was obtained which was in Maurice Johnson's collection bought from Sir Richard Ogle from the Duke of Suffolk. Maratt. p302.
5. Minutes of SGS 1724. Folio 78A. The Ailwyn coat of arms are drawn in and show various variations coloured blue, silver, sometimes with two black lions.
6. Maurice Johnson says they were in the uppermost windows of the north aisle next to the chancel in painted glass.
7. Maratt. P 304. Illustrations are down to someone else and they do not include a wheat sheaf or garb. So perhaps Mr. Maratt did not see the same bells.

Some early residents immortalised in stained glass. These fragments can be identified as parts of the arms of the following families: Ogle, Evington, Willesby, Dymoke, Welles, Engaine, Kyme, and Umfraville.

CHAPTER 11

AYSCOUGHFEE'S EARLY RESIDENTS

Continuously inhabited for nearly 600 years, with only minor alterations made during much of that time, Ayscoughfee is recognisably the same building that was home to the Ailwyn family in the fifteenth century. All the succession of residents have left their traces; a repair here, a new garden there, windows altered or remnants of their coats of arms in the stained glass.

Richard and Margaret Ailwyn may have lived here as they were Spalding people, which may have been long before the building of the new house, perhaps in a less grand timber house on the site. Opportunities to investigate signs of earlier buildings have been lost on two occasions; in 1959 when during the demolition the Gayton rubble was bulldozed into the cellars, and more recently when the ground floor at Ayscoughfee was partially removed. Now we shall probably never know.

The Ailwyns' eldest son, Nicholas, was born about 1435. The 15th century saw the beginning of building their new home, when the fortune that Richard has amassed enabled him to plan his grand new mansion. Perhaps the couple lived elsewhere during the construction. The year that their eldest son, Nicholas, went to London to start his apprenticeship with the Mercers was 1451, the same year the oaks were felled that would finally make the roof. So when the Ailwyn family duly took up residence of the newly built house, all their children were probably already born. When Margaret died and was buried in Spalding Parish Church, Nicholas took over with his new, nameless wife. Richard probably lived with them.

The Roundel may show old Richard, Nicholas, a child (perhaps Richard, born between 1471-1476), snuggling up to his mother. The clothes fit the date. By then, the Ailwyns enjoyed a grand life style; a large house, servants, lavish accommodation for many guests who were encouraged to stay by generous provisions, a large guest chamber, with the Roundel in a conspicuous place over the door to greet them at the entrance. This welcome Roundel is still in situ, but very worn now. If these calculations are correct,[1] the Roundel dates from mid to late 1470s, when the family were well installed and obviously determined to create an immediate impression.

In the Roundel, Richard looks relaxed, sitting comfortably holding his walking stick. He is the head of the family, being served by a page 'on the knee'. Nicholas became increasingly involved with his London business but made frequent home visits. He knew the road from Spalding to London like the back of his hand, still recalling the horrors of it at the end of his life in 1505. By then, Nicholas had married; nothing is known of his wife. Three more children, Joan and another girl and finally Fraunceys (an after thought?), born in 1492, but nothing is known of his wife's death, or of his father's except that they were both dead by 1505. His wife's death must have been after 1492 when Fraunceys was born. After a busy and fruitful life, at the end of January 1505/6, Nicholas died at his home in London, leaving Fraunceys, his youngest, as his immediate heir.

It is not safe to assume either that the house in Spalding was shut up or let out, or that Alice Hedge (who Nicholas appointed as custodian) was willing to leave the gaiety of London to live in the Fens, but he specified 'only if she was agreeable to so doing'.

As to Fraunceys's interest in Spalding (but he seems to have been centred in London), he had a wife called Bridget and lived in his father's house in Bow churchyard. He describes himself as a Mercer, but he was a bit of a failure, getting into debt and selling his father's property. After 1520 nothing can be found about him, but there were several actions for debt against him in 1518-20 and he may have survived.

If Alice Hedge was in charge in Spalding, as Nicholas considered her a most competent manager, everything would have been well looked after. There is no information about Nicholas, Richard's son, who was next in line. It all depended on Alice Hedge and her decision. There may be a hiatus here for probate was long delayed.

1. Although Dr Jonathan Clark thinks it is contemporary to the overall build date, around 1451.

Then the Hall family appeared. It would be nice to think of Alice continuing to keep the house in Spalding open. The Hall, Halle or Hawle family were well connected and appear to have come from Nottinghamshire, and they were the next to live at Ayscoughfee. As they acquired it in rather peculiar circumstances, I suspect there is more to this than we have as yet discovered.

The Halls of Spalding

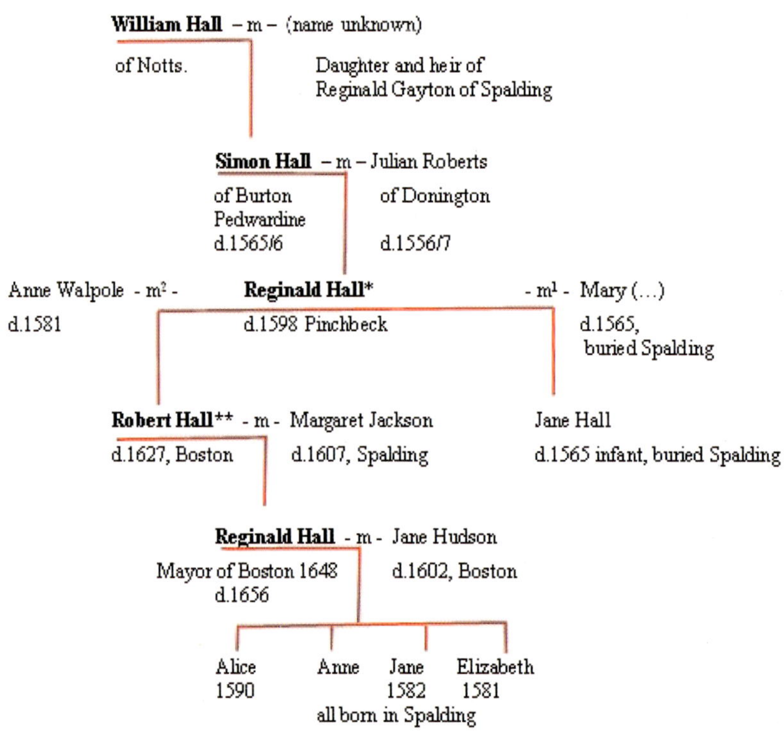

Reginald Hall was left Ayscoughfee by his mother, when she died in 1556. His grandmother was a Gayton of Spalding and his father Simon Hall. His mother was Juliana, Simon Hall's first wife. How Juliana Roberts obtained it is a puzzle that seems insoluble.

The large Hall clan with branches in Donnington, Greatford, Sharford, Westborough and Nottingham produced Commissioners for Sewers, MPs, a mayor of Boston, but Simon Hall who lived at Burton Pedwardine married an heiress from Donnington, Juliana Roberts, as his first wife. Little is known about the Roberts/Robinson family except that they were rich Boston merchants. How Juliana obtained Ayscoughfee, whether she bought it, was left it or ever lived there, is not revealed, but when she died Reginald, her son, inherited it; if Maddison is right, he was only thirteen. He was 23 when his father died, when his first wife died and was buried in Spalding. Buried in Pinchbeck, he died in 1598, after two more wives. All the Halls collected several wives.

His son, Robert, the child of Anne Walpole, his second wife, inherited Ayscoughfee and married Margaret Jackson in Spalding. As these Halls were married in Spalding, and the children of Reginald, his son, Anne, 1579, Jane, 1582, Elizabeth, 1581, were all buried in Spalding, there is a presumption they were then all living in Spalding before Reginald went to Boston to fame and fortune. Robert sold Ayscoughfee in 1602. The purchaser was Thomas Wimberley (or Wymberley).

Left, the Wimberley coat of arms

The Wimberleys were from Lancashire originally, settling in Bitchfield near Bourne, but then established in South Witham and Pinchbeck, although still describing themselves as of Bitchfield and Spalding. Thomas was born in 1555 and married to Frances Beville from Chesterton in Huntingdon, whose father was a knight. They are well documented and as many bits of misinformation have been relied on as there are spellings of their name. Frances Beville was related to the Gamlyn family of Spalding of Fulney Hall. Thomas and Frances were clearly upwardly mobile and were granted arms in 1588, just before their purchase of Ayscoughfee. The family lived there for two generations and they are an interesting family. Seven children were born to Frances and Thomas, Beville, Thomas, Elizabeth, William, John, Gilbert and Frances, all born between 1589 – 1594. Beville inherited Ayscoughfee upon his father's death in 1616. He married Elizabeth Wellby. Brother William is said to be a Royalist hero, who died of his wounds after the battle of Naseby. It is said he saved King Charles I's life in Smart Lane and then, severely wounded, managed to get home to South Witham where he died the next day (1605-1645). Unfortunately, he has been confused with his cousin William; our William was not the famous cavalier, but became a considerable landowner in his own right. The Wimberley family produced an unusual phenomenon in that three Wellby sisters married three Wimberley brothers. Family members had distinguished army careers in India and a later John Wimberley emigrated to Virginia, America in 1673.

Elizabeth née Wymberley inherited Ayscoughfee on the death of her brother Beville who died childless. Her father was obviously very fond of her and in his will she received a 'Gilded Bole' and a personal, meaningful gift of the ring he 'always wore'. She had by the time of her father's will two sons, Richard Evington (called after his grandfather), Maurice Evington and a daughter Franceys, and they all got varying sums of money.

Thomas Wimberley's will dated 1616 gives Frances, his wife, a life interest in the family lands in Spalding, Cowbit, Pinchbeck and Moulton and his ten acres in Barkers Row, Spalding. Beville received the house where he now dwells and other properties. Gilbert got twenty-six acres of pasture in Weston called Cowmedowe in the Queens Manor (perhaps Wimberley Hall, an Elizabethan manor, now demolished).

John got the lease in Bitchfield, leased from the Bishop of Lincoln. Beville is 'bound to accept and take kindly at his mother's hands for that he knoweth that by her good means and frugality she did provide the money which paid for them all'. Why should he fail to take kindly to the gift of Ayscoughfee? Was it perhaps too big for his needs?

Wimberley Hall, Weston. It's carved staircase is now in the Blackfriars Theatre, Boston.

Brother Gilbert, a graduate of Trinity College, Cambridge, became a cleric and Minister at St. Margaret's, Westminster, later a prebendary there. He also was Royalist and his valuable library was plundered by the Cromwellians. He died in 1653 but never recovered his books.

In 1618 Beville married Elizabeth Wellby who was the daughter of Sir William Wellby of Gedney K.B. They had no children. The Wellby family provided several other brides as John, Beville's brother, married Frances Wellby in 1625. This John started a new line of Wimberleys in Pinchbeck.

Beville died in 1641; his wife Elizabeth Wellby died soon after. His sister Elizabeth inherited Ayscoughfee and married in 1603 to Nicholas Evington in Spalding. He is described as 'of Spalding', but he had property in Pinchbeck and his family came from North Lincolnshire.

Beville Wimberley and Elizabeth Wellby did not continue to live at Ayscoughfee after 1616 until Beville's death in 1641; there were more changes. Elizabeth Evington married again in 1631 at St. Margaret's Westminster, to Dymoke Walpole of Pinchbeck. He had been married before in 1608 to Jane Ogle, daughter of Thomas Ogle of Pinchbeck.

Elizabeth née Wimberley married Nicholas Evington in 1603. They had six sons and one daughter. Married in Spalding, Nicholas came from an old North Lincolnshire family, another example of the emergence of wealthy families in Spalding during the 17th century. His father was Richard Evington and the family lived in a 14th century moated manor house, Halstead Hall. Nicholas was described as 'of Spalding'. The Evington coat of arms may give some clues about them.

Digitally enhanced restoration of the Evington coat of arms found in the bay window at Ayscoughfee.

1. John Wimberley, a 'gentleman of Pinchbeck and Bychfield' received a grant of 400 acres of land in Nansemond County, Virginia and had permission to transport 7 persons to America including his son John, 18 at the time, and his household. They formed a large, thriving branch of the Wimberleys, spread all over America. See *Wimberley Family Lineage* (1987) Karen Newforth and Thomas C. Wimberley.
2. Probate granted 29th May 1616.

During the currency of the marriage between Elizabeth and Nicholas Evington in 1621, it seems that the Evingtons were not living at Ayscoughfee, as Beville was still alive and Elizabeth did not inherit until Beville's death in 1641. Sensibly, an exchange was arranged, but before that Beville and Elizabeth, his wife, went to Pinchbeck while the Evingtons moved into Ayscoughfee. Beville and Elizabeth were childless, while the Evingtons had seven children.

On the 16th April 1621 two conveyances of identical date recorded this exchange and Nicholas, who had been brought up in some grandeur at Halstead, found himself owner of Ayscoughfee where he would have felt entirely at home. The house and five acres were swapped for a capital messuage in Pinchbeck, together with thirty-one acres of land and pasture.

A great deal of research has gone into establishing the site of the Evington household in Pinchbeck. Nicholas Evington is recorded in 1617 as a landowner in Pinchbeck,[1] of the manor of Wekys, Wikes or Wakes, but so far no further identification has been possible. So when Elizabeth inherited she was already living at Ayscoughfee, and continued to do so until Nicholas' death in 1630. In 1631 she remarried, this time to Dymoke Walpole, and in 1639, as her son John Evington had inherited the house on the death of his father, Dymoke Walpole bought it from her. Elizabeth Wimberley, then Evington, now Walpole, stayed at Ayscoughfee after her marriage at Westminster on 27th October 1631 to Dymoke Walpole.

Walpole Arms: "*Or, on a fesse between two chevrons, sable three cross crosslets argent*"

He was the sixth son of Arthur Walpole and his wife Susan Dymoke of Scrivelsby. The oldest sons of the Dymoke family of Scrivelsby are, by long tradition, the Kings Champion, whose function is to ride on his charger in full armour into the coronation feast for a new monarch at St. Stephen's Hall. He invites challenges from anyone who questions the right of the new King. This tradition goes back to the time of Richard II.

These Walpoles came from Pinchbeck. Elizabeth and Dymoke's son became Sir John Walpole, when Dymoke died in 1642. Gooch says Elizabeth then retired to Louth where she died in 1649 (some say 1642 and that she was buried in Spalding).

Before the next inhabitants are introduced during the stay of the Evington family, there was a time when two of the Evington family lived at Ayscoughfee and divided the manor into two by building a partition across the great hall. The two halves of the divided hall then had separate chimneys installed. There is still visual evidence of this in the roof timbers. The great hall was probably reinstated as one room in 1639.

Nicholas Evington's will in 1630 leaves only a life interest in Ayscoughfee to Elizabeth, which would end if she remarries. In that event, the house is left to his brother Morris and after that to John, his youngest son. Oddly, John only retains the house for a limited period 'until he shall have beyond the sum of £500 from all the profits thereof' and then the house goes to Morris his brother and then back to John.

Exactly how and when both John and Morris lived there, in a divided house, is not revealed but in 1639 John sold it to his step father, Dymoke Walpole, and he and Elizabeth moved back in.

Dymoke could not have been a young man as he had been married to Jane Ogle of Pinchbeck, and they had produced nine sons and five daughters. John Walpole, the eldest son of Dymoke and Jane Ogle, born in 1612, entered Grays Inn intending to become a barrister but went instead to fight for the King, becoming the standard bearer to Charles I and a cornet of the King's Troop. He must have been on good terms with Charles I for he knighted him at Cardiff on 31st July 1645.

1. The numerous manors of Pinchbeck, at least nine, seem to change their names and their owners with confusing regularity.

He continued to be a Royalist and suffered accordingly, having to pay £450 during the Protectorate to compound his estates, one of the small groups of Royalists in Spalding ordered to do so.[1] He was still alive at the Restoration and became standard bearer to the new King. By 1672 he is recorded as living in London, and he died in August 1672 and was buried at Windsor Castle. The Walpoles continued in Pinchbeck, lived in Walpole Hall,[2] a very grand Tudor house. Edward Walpole's tomb[3] in the chancel marks the grave of Edward Walpole, who died on 14th February 1725 and as Walpole Hall is now demolished, his grave is the only memorial.

Next on the scene were the Johnsons who purchased Ayscoughfee in 1658. John Johnson also came from Pinchbeck. They were the first Johnsons and no relation of the more famous second family of Johnsons who lived at Ayscoughfee for six generations.

The Rutland Johnsons

The first Johnsons came from Lincolnshire and the question arises as to whether they are the same Johnsons as the Johnsons of Rutland (the founder of Uppingham and Oakham schools). The Johnson family of Rutland had a coat of arms identical with these Johnsons. Morris Johnson was an Alderman of Stamford, whose son, Robert Johnson, became Archdeacon of Leicester and founded Uppingham and Oakham schools in about 1584. He was the parson of North Luffenham. As they seem to share identical coats with the Johnsons of Pinchbeck it can be reasonably assumed they are connected.

John Johnson was married to the daughter of Sir Robert Ogle, also of Pinchbeck, another Royalist family. Jane had four children, Francis, Dorothy, John and another John, all born between 1638 and 1650, when Jane died in childbirth. The Ogle family are represented on the Johnson family coat of arms. The Ogles were originally an important family from Northumberland, who held a barony granted in 1461, and were connected to only great families, including the Devonshires and Shrewsburys.

The Ogle Coat of Arms

The barony went into abeyance in 1691 and is now most probably extinct. The Ogles were stewards of Spalding and one of them was clerk to Crowland Abbey, but Sir Richard Ogle was described as Lord of Pinchbeck. Again, the manor is confusing, it is described as Bonds, Bounds or even Bonsd, but it seems that this was the Ogle Manor and Hall, which included a mansion which is on the site of one of the present halls, now rebuilt. Thomas Ogle, last of the line for the barony, died in Fleet prison in 1627. Richard Ogle had a house in Spalding[4] and held ninety-eight acres in 1619 with seven other houses. The son of Jane and John Johnson (born 1638), Francis (who married Jane Green), inherited on the death of John and they had three children, John, Jane and Isabella. Isabella married Colonel Adrian Gamlyn and died young, and John did not survive. Jane was left sole heiress.

1. Rosalyn Pursglove quoting '*Ayscoughfee and its owners*'. Jennifer Vernon. Unpublished thesis.
2. Robin Harmstone describes Otway or Pinchbeck Hall as 'a large building, erected about the time of Henry VIII, moated, some windows having pointed lights and square heads, with lofty chimneys with spire shaped ornaments on the gable ends at the sides, each crowned with an ornamental ball'. Only Otway House is marked on the Ordnance Survey and much more research is needed to identify the various manors and houses.
3. Pevsner (Lincolnshire) singles out this tomb and describes it as a boldly moulded sarcophagus with an unusual peaked top in Pinchbeck church.
4. Robin Harmstone. P2.

One family of Johnsons followed another. In 1683, Jane married Maurice Johnson (no relation) and two years later John Johnson, her father, died. On the death of her father she inherited everything. So Jane became Lady of Ayscoughfee. She had eight children and after her death in 1703 Maurice went on to marry Elizabeth Oldfield and Anne Wood. Through her, Maurice Johnson [1] became sole owner of Ayscoughfee because women could not hold property in their own right. His last wife, who he married at Southwick on 11th February 1618, had been 'woman to Dame Bridget Gamlyn, wife of Sir John Gamlyn of Fulney Hall'. They had twelve children, but only five survived. Martin and Walter became masters of the Grammar School, John Johnson became clerk to the Court of Sewers, and the fourth, William, became Registrar of the Ecclesiastical Court at Bedford. Afterwards, Walter, born 1619, became an attorney and Justice of the Peace. He was also a Captain of the Trained Bands[1] and always known as Captain Johnson. The Johnsons had moved up the social scale.

Walter was the on the last rung of the ladder of progress of the Johnson family. In 1685, the Johnsons acquired Ayscoughfee on Jane's father's death, the first Maurice was a barrister and Captain of Holland Foot, and they were the second Johnsons at Ayscoughfee. Of his three wives, Elizabeth Oldfield, Ann Wood of Boston, he had seven children but only two survived.

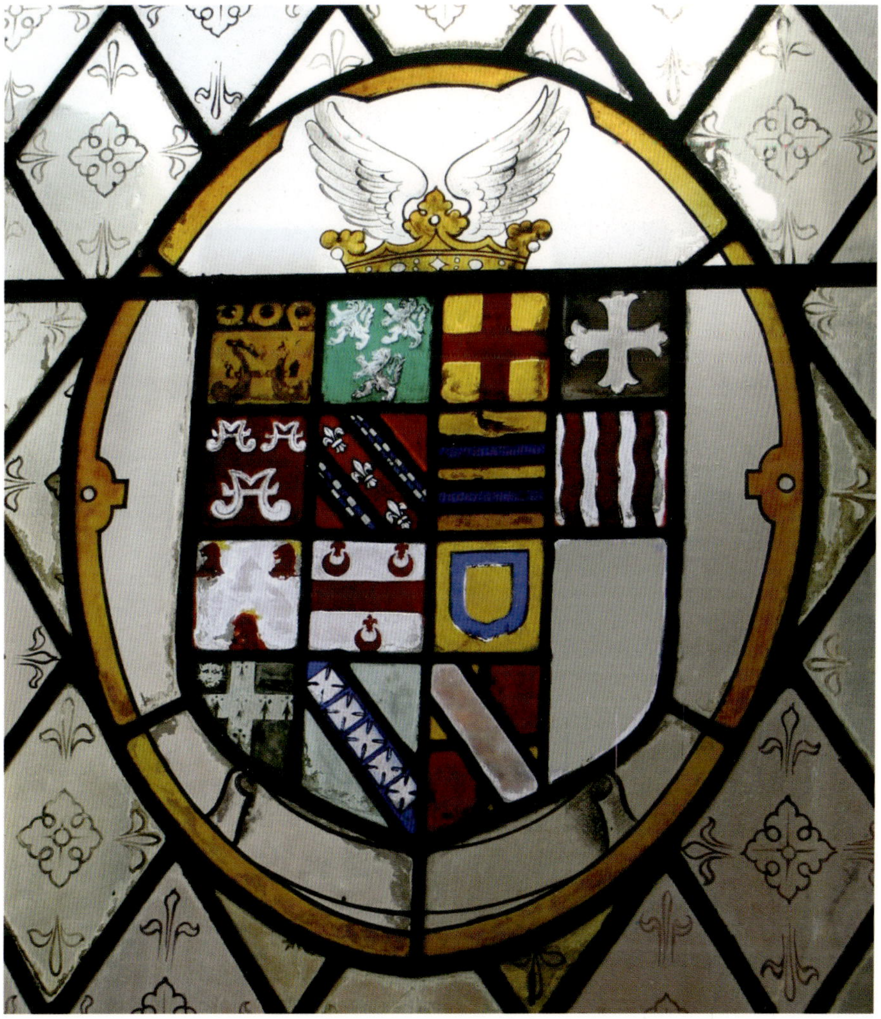

The Johnson Coat of Arms. Detail from the window on the landing in the North Wing. From top left to bottom right:

1. Johnson of Spalding	**2. Tyson, Thane of Alnwick**	**3. Fitzjohn**	**4. De Vesci**
5. Rousse of Grimolsby	**6. Wingfield**	**7. St Martyn**	**8. Downes**
9. Johnson of Pinchbeck	**10. Ogle**	**11. Bartram**	**12. Pinchbeck (missing)**
13. Ambler	**14. Atkirk**	**15. Lessington**	**16. Thorpe (missing)**

Sources: Maurice Johnson – notebook. Description of Topaz Seal, and the Hatchment of Theophilus Johnson (1826-92) in the Parish Church

1. Gooch claims that this branch of the family left Spalding, leaving only Walter.

CHAPTER 12

THE JOHNSONS OF AYSCOUGHFEE

The scene was set. Now a leading Spalding family with legal connections, a large and grand house, money to spend on a good education at Spalding Grammar School, the Johnsons lived in Ayscoughfee, and had become a strong family with loving parents. There, in 1688, Maurice (the Antiquary) was born, the eldest of the family, born with a crested silver spoon in his mouth.

Maurice Johnson [2] in 1731 by George Vertue.
The original is in the National Portrait Gallery

Maurice the Antiquary was probably the most important man that Spalding ever produced. After a sound and thorough education in the Classic languages, he was admitted to the Inner Temple on 26th May 1705, and was called to the Bar on 26th January 1710, aged twenty two. At this age, he started practice as circuiteer from chambers in London, spending time at Assizes at Ely and Wisbech and London courts in term time.

When his father died in 1747 (the first Maurice) he inherited Ayscoughfee and by this time he was married to 'the girl next door', Elizabeth Ambler, with whom he spent a very contented married life. She gave birth to twenty-six children (several twins) and twelve of them survived to reach maturity and were able to sit round the dining table together. They were a close and united family; his sons followed him in his pursuits and family letters show parental concern and affection for their large brood. All his life, he was an enthusiastic, avid collector. He was concerned with all sorts of antiquities and interested in everything medical, botanic, geological, astral and literary.

He loved coins, gems, stained glass and enjoyed art, music, dancing and all oddities. All finds by himself and his many friends were meticulously recorded in his Minute Books, still held on their premises by the Spalding Gentlemen's Society. But he did not keep all this knowledge and information to himself, but shared it with his many friends in Lincoln, Peterborough, Stamford, Boston, Oundle, Wisbech and, of course, his legal friends on circuit and in London. He was immensely sociable and was drawn to meet his friends and exchange views in a coffeehouse (Buttons). When in Spalding, he missed this and in 1709 he organised one meeting 'on trial' in a coffeehouse.

His weekly meetings caught on and attracted firstly local people and over the years many notabilities showed interest. When it first started to meet, it had modest aims. London papers arrived by coach and on coaching day the Tatler was read aloud (not because the members were illiterate but because there was only one copy). In London, he and his barrister friends met at Buttons coffeehouse to drink coffee, and in Spalding they met at Younger's coffeehouse in the Abbey yard. As he himself said, he led a busy life which involved a great deal of travelling, but he managed to attend most of the meetings of the Gentlemen's Society, of which he was the founder and moving spirit.[1] "I constantly attended meetings whether in London at term time or on the Midland circuit or attending the Isle of Ely Assize, there or at Wisbech, I too came to communicate something literary to every meeting".[2]

1. Maurice's own account of how it all started written late in life. pIX of Introduction.
2. Before the amalgamation with the Oxford circuit combining Aylesbury, Bedford, Northampton, Lincoln, Leicester, Nottingham, Birmingham and Stafford with the Midland circuit.

He remained Secretary for thirty-five years and then became President for the rest of his life. After its modest formation in 1709 the Spalding Gentlemen's Society had various homes. In 1743 they moved to a permanent home in Gayton House[1] (Holyrood House), where they stayed until 1755 when Maurice died (Gayton, of course, belonged to Maurice). They met in a house near High Bridge (over Mr. Cox's apothecary shop) after a stay at a place in Abbey buildings. Finally, they built themselves custom built premises in Broad Street.

Maurice was also keenly interested in his own family history and at the top of the stairs at Ayscoughfee a stained glass panel shows all his family connections, Amblers, Ogles and the other Johnsons, several as yet untraced. (see P57)

The glass of the window shows his ties with Taillbois, Umfraville, Dymoke, Welles and Oldfield. A collection of Johnson Hatchments in the Parish Church and the tombs there are of great interest.[2] Part of the Parish Church has almost become a Johnson mausoleum. But a tomb to Maurice himself there has never been.[3] He also recalls discovering a most unusual seal in the form of a topaz cut in the form of the Johnsons' coat of arms. "My kinsman, Sir Henry Johnson" owned it and he had a handsome seat at Great Berkhamstead and all sorts of noble relations. The Johnsons of Norfolk are connected but it is not obvious where they fit in and may be the family of William the ecclesiastical registrar, who he refers to as "Great Uncle William".[4]

As the Johnson family are the real genus of Ayscoughfee, with their apotheosis in Maurice [2] the Antiquary, a little could be said about his ancestors. The glass window showing all his ancestors speaks for itself. The number and spread of their family connections deserves much more consideration that there is room for here. Gooch claims the Johnsons came from Sutterton and that Martin (the first recorded Johnson) was an attorney and was the father of Ben Johnson,[5] the actor and dramatist. His first son, another Martin, born in 1588, came to Spalding at the beginning of the 17th century and was married three times to Eleanor, Elizabeth and Jane Lynne of Southwick Hall.

The young Maurice [2] continued to practice at the Bar but there is no way to discover how successful he was. He had the requisite qualities; he could talk well, write good prose, was extremely popular and persuasive. As to his physical appearance, the miniature of him as a young man shows a young, intelligent face almost overwhelmed by a large and shaggy wig. He looks slightly built, but he must have been extremely tough. The time came when he had more calls on his time in Lincolnshire but he seemed to be keeping all his options open as well as devoting much time and energy to his new society.

In due course he became steward to the Duke of Buccleuch for his manor of Spalding, as well as steward to the Earl of Exeter at Kirton. He may have taken these posts over from his father after his death in 1747. He also became Chairman of South Holland Quarter Sessions (held at Spalding) and Deputy Recorder at Stamford Quarter Sessions.

The source of his problems with his balance which bedevilled his later life were not diagnosed and may have been caused by a number of different factors.

---

1. In May 1743, SGS Minute Book records their acceptance of the secretary's offer of 'part of the Mansion House of the late Mr. Ambler' with accommodation for the co-adjutor (caretaker), a museum and parlour, secretary's and treasurer's offices, and with use of the cellar and the use of the courtyard for their garden.
2. Jane Johnson has a poem on her tombstone. She died aged 37 in 1703 and Elizabeth Johnson is remembered by a mournful statue; she died in 1843.
3. His grave and memorial slab are now discovered well concealed under the pews and not inspectable.
4. Minute Book p17. William was the son of the second Martin Johnson, who became a distinguished cleric, LLD and registrar of the ecclesiastical court at Bedford, and was a learned lawyer and poet. Archbishop Juxon appointed him a Notary Public in 1661 while he was Archbishop of Canterbury.
5. Gooch claims he was baptized on 26th March 1574 at Sutterton (p202) but there seems no support for this. His dates are given as 1665-1742 (DNB). Another branch of the same family also claim him, and maintain he was Poet Laureate to James I.

His son Maurice [3] (1714-1793), always known as the Colonel, because of his military career, took over upon his death. He appears to have been married twice and had five children[1] (Maurice [4] was Rector of Spalding and married Anne Buckworth, daughter of Theophilus Buckworth of Clay Hall). Maurice [4] (1756-1834) was a cleric, attending St. John College, Cambridge and becoming Curate of Moulton. His wife, Frances, died giving birth to Maurice [5] in 1815 and her husband died in 1820. Maurice [5] was brought up by his grandparents at Ayscoughfee and in due course inherited from his grandfather.

Major Maurice [6] (1815-1864) married Elizabeth Mills in 1841 but she died in 1843, and in 1848 he married Isabella Swann. They had three little girls, Mary, Frances and Alethea and after the tragic death of Frances in 1850 they decided to move to Suffolk and after the birth of two more daughters, Edith and Frances they settled at Blundeston.

Portraits of Maurice Johnson [6] and Isabella, and right, Elizabeth Johnson's memorial

PIC-NICS IN AYSCOUGHFEE PADDOCK – During the past week, the first of the holidays, the recreation ground at Ayscoughfee has been resorted to by hundreds of children daily: and it has been an interesting and refreshing spectacle to see them revelling in the enjoyments of the field, away from the dangers of the street. Each day, too, during the afternoon, a considerable number of little knots of children have spread themselves upon the grass and have taken tea together pic-nic fashion. Mrs. Walker, of the Hall, has supplied the children with boiling water, and right heartily they have enjoyed themselves. Of late too, parties of adults have frequently taken tea together on the lawn. In a word, old and young alike are immensely appreciating the advantages of ayscoughfee

Free Press article from 1898

In 1851 the last of the six Johnson families left Ayscoughfee. The census of that year shows Maurice as 'landed proprietor' and for he and his wife and one young daughter, he had ten servants. They finally settled in Suffolk, where Maurice died in 1864. His wife survived him for twenty years. The Johnsons left Ayscoughfee and a succession of tenants took over. Mr. Wright was followed by Mr. Parke[2] and then Mr. Henry Hawkes in 1865 was there for about five years. He was a member of the well known Quaker family, who owned and lived in Welland Hall. In 1868, Ayscoughfee was advertised as for let as a 'family mansion with extensive grounds'.

1. Some say he married Mary Bates, some Mary Baker, who was his maid. This may be why he moved to Stanway, only returning to Ayscoughfee on Mary's death in 1773. She gave birth to Maurice in 1755. It was this Colonel Johnson that the Hon. John Byng visited in 1790, where his two daughters were drying roses.
2. (Gooch). Miss Parke, his sister, always went across the road to church in a sedan chair, carried by estate gardeners. It had blinds for privacy and now stands downstairs in the SGS museum. All sorts of practical jokes were played upon her, resulting in an indignant Miss Parke having to walk home.

A well known local solicitor, Mr. Charles Foster Bonner, occupied the Hall from 1874 until 1896, with his wife and two offspring and four domestic servants, including a man servant.[1] He is said to be responsible for building the garden room. It was obvious the widow of the last Johnson, Isabella, who had settled in Suffolk, would never return to Ayscoughfee. She decided to sell.

AYSCOUGHFEE HALL AND GARDENS.

THE WHIT-MONDAY PUBLIC OPENING---TREAT TO THE OLD FOLKS.

AYSCOUGHFEE HALL—SPALDING'S JUBILEE MEMORIAL

Above: Lincolnshire, Boston, and Spalding Free Press, April 1898

A WELCOME GIFT TO AYSCOUGHFEE - Two welcome announcements were made by the Chairman (Mr. S. Kingston) at a meeting of the Ayscoughfee Committee on Friday night. The first was that Mrs. Johnson – who had disposed of Ayscoughfee to the town on such favourable terms – had presented two valuable paintings, portraits of her late husband and herself, to be hung in Ayscoughfee Hall. Mr. Kingston was requested to cordially thank Mrs. Johnson for her generous gift, and the opinion was expressed that other similar presents would follow. It was also stated that a cheque for £39 10s. had been received from the Athletic Sports Committee, under the terms of the agreement in respect of the Bank Holiday hire of the gardens and grounds. It was reported that the Recreation Ground was very largely visited by the children, and was much appreciated. Matters were also considered in connection with the closing fête of the season on the 8th September. A most attractive programme is being organised, and there is every probability that the event will excite a good deal of interest.

Free Press article from 1898

In 1898 the long drawn out negotiations making the Hall over to a committee of Spalding citizens, who later made the Hall over to Spalding Urban District Council, were completed and the price of £2100 was paid over. In 1902 the house was finally presented to the people of Spalding as a celebration of the coronation of Edward VII in 1902.

Isabella Johnson and her husband's portraits now hang at Ayscoughfee in commemoration of her gift.

1. 1891 Census.

The Hall was now available for all sorts of new uses – the idea of a free library was vetoed locally although a grant from the Carnegie Trust was offered. In 1920, a private school (now at Welland Hall) was started at Ayscoughfee; it remained there until 1981.

The era of the public library finally came to Spalding at Ayscoughfee in 1937, and it remained there until the premises in Victoria Street were opened in 1966.

During the first World War, the War Office took over the house and housed Belgian refugees[1] there. During the second, Land Army (women land workers were housed there) and a stray bomb fell in the gardens, when most of the windows (including the stained glass) were broken but carefully retained and reformed. The damage to the building was not great.

Bowling at Ayscoughfee in the 1950s, a popular pastime in the gardens since 1908

In 1951 the famous bird collection belonging to Ashley Maples was moved to Ayscoughfee from premises in Red Lion Street. This was a great attraction but unfortunately Spalding has now lost it all to Leicester Museum, for all sorts of unsatisfactory reasons; generations of Spalding children remember the amazing birds.

In 1974 the South Holland District Council who took over from Spalding Urban District Council decided that Ayscoughfee should become a museum. Since then various displays have been developed – the Drainage Exhibition, the Bird Collection, the Art Gallery, the scenes of life in South Holland, and two galleries on Spalding history and the history of Ayscoughfee. Finally, the exhibition for Matthew Flinders of Donnington was opened.

In 2002, all this was swept away and the building was emptied and closed, and the key handed over to the temporary custodians. A grant from the Lottery Fund was topped up by money from South Holland District Council and Lincolnshire Tourism and the Friends of Ayscoughfee. The restoration took four years, bringing in many experts in all sorts of fields from dendrochronology to stained glass, and lead roofing to decorative plaster work. Anderson and Glenn were appointed Project Managers and Conservation Architects and worked under the overall management of South Holland District Council.

On 30th June 2006 the restored Ayscoughfee was formally reopened by Dr. Jonathan Clark and the rest is history.

1. See page with postcard.

CHAPTER 13

THE STAINED GLASS AT AYSCOUGHFEE

The collection of medieval glass at Ayscoughfee[1] is now displayed in the top half of the full-height bay window in the great hall. Looking at it from the gallery where it is just a few feet away, when the sun is shining through it, is an amazing sight. The colours are jewel-like, all the hues of the rainbow, deep glowing red, royal blue, a bright fresh green, black and gold. Even the jumbled up pieces light up.

Maurice Johnson [2], the Antiquary was an avid collector and the collection has had an interesting career, being moved about, but even now the collection is not complete. Some of it was formerly in the oratory, some in a front window at Ayscoughfee. The Flemish roundels are still housed by the Spalding Gentlemen's Society. During the last War, a stray bomb hit Ayscoughfee and shattered the windows, but every single piece was collected and put together again. There is no complete window telling bible stories or portraying saints, or serialising scenes from the Bible, but then they probably were not complete when Maurice Johnson acquired them.

The glass, French, Flemish and English, spans five centuries. There is a kaleidoscope of pieces, hundreds of them, some jumbled, and most of them telling a story; three panels contain heraldry of many Lincolnshire families, including a Maurice Johnson family tree in glass (in the window at the top of the stairs), besides many reassembled scenes. The background of all panels are not from a church but secular; funny little 15th century birds of all kinds, with human expressions. A very similar 15th century set of birds was in a public house in Yarnton, Oxon, but now is in St. Bartholomew's Church at Yarnton. The other scenes have a quasi-religious connotation.

The Marriage Scene
This is in the centre panel of the middle of the bay window, and is French. Part of a French series of seven sacraments from 1500. The priest joins the hands of the young couple.

She is attended by two bridesmaids in yellow and green, while she is in silver and gold. The very young bridegroom has a deep crimson outfit with fur collar and golden slippers.

1. Tattershall has much medieval 15th century glass. York Minster has some 12th century panels (see Medieval Glass, the Pitkin Guide).

The oldest pieces are the two expressive faces below the marriage scene. The unhappy looking Virgin, in a hood with her curly hair showing is late 13th century, as is the beardless young man, who is probably St. John.

The gentleman holding up the roof and holding an orb with spiders behind him is early 14th century, all English.

Below, the two horrors are probably torturers, helping the damned to hell. They are of English origin.

Coronation of the Virgin

This features the enthroned Christ, robed in red with an orb. He crowns the Virgin who is wearing a white robe with a blue cloak. Christ's head has been replaced with the rather plain face of an angel. French, early 16th century.

The Banqueting Scene
Situated at the bottom of the left -hand window, is a little jumbled but the King can be identified because he has a golden crown (this piece is out of place as he is on the floor) but the food on the table is on golden dishes and goblets are clear.

There is a flower arrangement. The host, wearing a black beret, looks apprehensive, perhaps because a baby has landed in his arms and a goat with golden horns has appeared.

There is a lady in a headdress with her back to her host, and two men with caps.

One is looking away, appearing displeased (his hands are not part of this scene). This glass was made in the early 16th century and may be French.

Maurice Johnson mentions the glass at Ayscoughfee and his collection when he wrote a paper (*No. 10, a Heraldry in Glass Engraving and Painting*). He was most knowledgeable and wrote treatises on glass making and the history of it, and he says:

"Of the painted glass in my house, the Coats of Arms before being put again in my hall are shown with some others collected by me since, of some principal families in this county."

He goes on to describe places where the glass is particularly fine; Lincoln Cathedral, Lincoln Inns Chapel and the Inns of Court in London, and Kings College Cambridge:

"As they were done about the time of my historical pieces, the Host of Heaven, the showing of the wound and the sacraments of confirmation and marriage[1] (probably Henry V and Katherine, Princess of France) were at the expence of Mr. Ailwyn (a wealthy merchant who rebuilt my home) and perhaps painted by the same hand."

The history of glass making and the stories from these three panels would fill a book, and more. The heraldry included with them is an extra bonus. It is a huge jigsaw but the arms of the families of Oldfield, Bell, Ogle, Irby, Evington, Hall, Russell, Dymoke, Johnson of Pinchbeck, Pinchbeck, Taillbois and Welles families are all to be found in the three panels.

1. These scenes are now in the bay window, except the confirmation, and Maurice confirms they were in the house before his arrival.

Digitally restored heraldic images of a squirrel and coney (rabbit) from Ayscoughfee. The squirrel is a period charge, found in the grant of arms to the (now-defunct) *Worshipful Company of Grey Tawyers* (ie tanners) in 1476

The medieval glass in Tattershall Church – or what is left of it – has some similarities with Ayscoughfee. In the new Collegiate Church rebuilt by Ralph, Lord Cromwell in 1440, the windows were ablaze with the glowing colours of the painted glass. These depicted, in series, stories from the Old and New Testaments, the Magnificat, and the lives of the Saints. It was finally completed in 1482.

Example of the Tattershall glass

They were much admired by most people, but in 1737 the vicar complained that the glass made the church to dark to see to read, but nothing was done immediately. No-one took this seriously, and forgot about it until 1754, when the then Lord of the Manor came to an agreement with the Earl of Exeter, who promised £50 for the glass, and to replace it with clear panes. Suspecting that this would cause outrage, the village enlisted the help of Joseph Banks, of Revesby. They secretly removed the glass under the cover of darkness, breaking quite a lot of it in the process.

The Earl of Exeter made a feeble attempt to put things right and to replace the glass in the nave, but nothing was done and the chancel was left windowless for fifty years. The Parish Register of 1757 records the expenditure on sixty-two dozen glass squares, at 4d per dozen, and in the next year Mr. Stephenson was paid 10/- and 17/6 for glazing work.

The bits left broken were carefully put together, and replaced, but the result is a terrible jumble. The lost glass is now at Burghley, Warwick Castle, and St. Martin's Church, Stamford.

CHAPTER 14

PANORAMA

This chapter shows a pictorial progression of the changes to Ayscoughfee over the centuries.

The Oak Panel - Probably the oldest image of Ayscoughfee, the nearest to its original appearance.

From the Spalding Gentlemen's Society collection (undated)

This picture, never published before, is just one section of a large wooden panel, approximately six feet wide and two feet tall, and is currently displayed in the SGS Museum. The panel shows the riverside panorama from High Bridge to Ayscoughfee, and is centred on Gayton House.

The view of Ayscoughfee shows plain gabled cross wings, a slate roof, no chimneys, and no visible door at the front. No sign of the kitchen buildings on the south, a loop instead of the bay window, two windows only are plain, six panes. The yew tree arches are still small. There is a low front wall with a gate on the south side. The north extension has one chimney, continual string courses, staircase tower, octagonal and low, square tower has moulded stone windows and ground floor door at side. The north extension view shown here is almost exactly as it looks now except for the chimneys and the top of the tower, and there is now no outside door visible to basement. The building looks quite homely and not very grand. As this representation is fairly accurate, the mystery lies in the complete absence of the front bay window, which appears to be hidden by the north wing. The panel cannot be easily dated, but the bridge and church clock are the best keys.

High Bridge (left) has stout, wooden palisaded sides, installed in about 1550. This stone bridge with four arches, was demolished and replaced with a wooden structure sometime in the 1600s, and Vermuiden noted in 1642 that the central pillar had been "lately removed" when the river was widened.

The panel was at Ayscoughfee before its removal to SGS, but it could have just have easily been commissioned to decorate Gayton House.

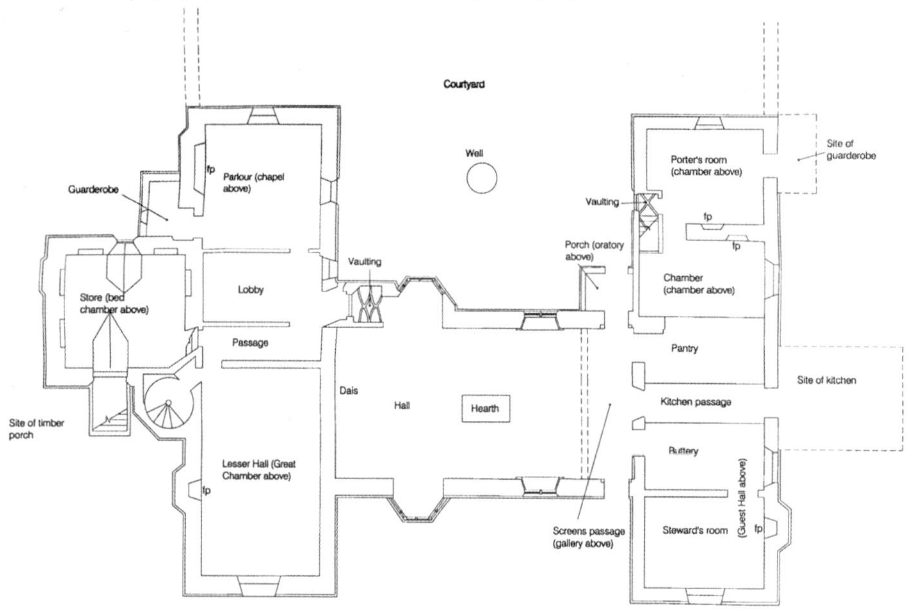

fp fireplace

Conjectured plan of Ayscoughfee Hall in the 15th century	Scale 1:125	Figure 17

FIELD ARCHAEOLOGY SPECIALISTS - HISTORIC BUILDINGS SECTION

Both Figures: Historic Buildings Assessment, 2005

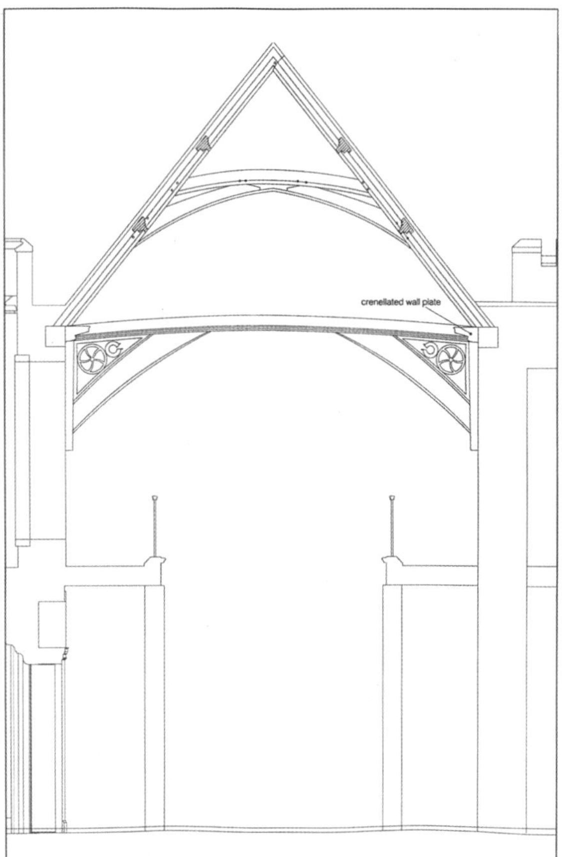

Indicative section showing hall roof truss form at the south end	Scale 1:50	Figure 13

FIELD ARCHAEOLOGY SPECIALISTS - HISTORIC BUILDINGS SECTION

Inside - no picture shows the interior or the back at this time, but the hall stretched full length between the wings. This hall was the living area. The great hall spread out with the oak roof exposed, with carving showing on the spandrels. The front and rear entrance doors were joined by a screens passage at the southern end of the great hall. The kitchen would have been a separate building because of the fire risks. In the south wing there was a second floor with large chambers, accommodation for guests with its own staircase and entry stairway. The north wing, also two storeys, had a large room on the ground floor and a staircase in the turret and a large bedroom above for the lord, with his own private outside door, with handrail and stone staircase, like Tattershall. There was little privacy, space was at a premium, privacy a luxury. The small room (oratory) over the back porch still there and can be seen. Each room had a specific function, not that they were always clear. Several Garderobes were provided and water from a well outside. Very large numbers of staff and retainers lived in, probably sleeping in the hall, while the female maids had a separate room in the north wing.

Left, the carved spandrels and details of the main roof

The photograph above, shows the detail of one of the spandrels of the roof of the Great Hall at Ayscoughfee. Note how plain it looks compared to the carved dragons at Dragon Hall. The photograph below is looking towards the same area of removed ceiling.

The Nattes Drawings - These two fine pencil sketches were commissioned by Joseph Banks in 1791 from John Claude Nattes (1765-1822). They are now in the Banks Collection at Lincoln Central Library.

The front of Ayscoughfee in 1791

A chimney stack is now shown on the south cross wing, and the one of the north wing has remained, but the tower and the turret are not shown. The yew hedge has grown and is neatly clipped and the middle is now an arch. The two windows have been replaced by four, with moulded tops and diamond panes, long narrow frames, almost grouped like lancets. The ground floor south window is now barred. Windows have appeared in the side of the north wing and on the ground floor. The front door has now moved one bay to the north and has a large window over it. This means that the screens passage has been removed by this point – probably during the time of the Evingtons.[1] The bay window has diamond panes, and there are drainpipes with large hoppers.

Rear view – this is the earliest recorded view of the back of the house.

It is neatly fenced and gated, and already has the appearance of having been extended. There are large windows, all different in style, the bedrooms have large square panes and a third floor attic has a small window. Three lots of drainpipes appear intrusive but are seen to drain into a tub. There is a back door under a small porch roof with a tall window above it, which has diamond framed glass and an oddly shaped bay with the same glass. The north wing is not clearly drawn and the tower hardly appears at all, just peeping over the roof line. The dog-toothed edge of the roof remains on back and front.

1. See Dr. Jonathan Clark's comments on page 11 of the HBA.

As far as is known, it was at the end of the eighteenth century that the great hall had a ceiling installed to create an impressive entrance hall, as at Althorp. The first floor galleries were created and Georgian (Adamesque) decoration installed throughout. A great deal of lead-work was also installed or restored at this time.

Detail from the lead cistern displayed in the hall showing one of the Johnson motifs. These are also shown on the recently restored rain-water hoppers that date from 1794. Similar hoppers ones can be seen on the Nattes drawings.

The Everard Watercolour - This sketch is by a young artist (14 year old) R.Everard and was bought by SHDC in 2005. It was drawn 'from the spot' in about 1800, during the residence of Maurice Johnson DD.

It shows the new railings, the gates, the landscaped garden and that the yew hedge has been removed and replaced by two pots. The clothes look like 1800, and the painting is very detailed, showing the tower with a jaunty flag, the chimney and another side chimney in use. The bay window has gone, a new front central door has appeared, all the windows have been altered and for the first time a triangular pediment has appeared with nine new windows where there were none before. The front facing door has appeared, and creepers are well established. All the front windows have curved tops and square panes. At least one of these windows survives, and can be seen in the upstairs room in the north range. This is undated but Dr. Johnson took over Ayscoughfee on the death of his father in 1793, so it could be any time after that. All the windows are new and different, they all match each other, and the door in the tower has finally appeared, finials on the front gables and a neatly manicured v-shaped lawn with railings and gates. Only a short time after the Nattes painting, the new owners have changed a lot and the tall finials are here to stay.

The 1808 Storer Engraving

This miniature, dating from 1808, is by William Brand, and engraved by James Storer, (1771-1853) who was noted for the extreme accuracy of his work. This illustration was produced for the Antiquarian and Topographical Cabinet (1807-11). It shows very much the same scene as the Everard painting, except here the garden look smaller and nearer the river. The front door is shown as having a rounded porch with wooden supports and the windows are clearly shown in timber with gothic tracery. The turret still has a flag but the tower now has drain pipes (the hoppers are dated '1794') and the tall chimney remains, together with the pointed finials, which look larger and more pronounced. The corners of the gables seem to have been slightly altered. A castellated pediment containing a semi-circular window is unaltered, although drawn slightly differently.

The Burgess Miniatures (with acknowledgement to Spalding Gentlemen's Society)

The Front - This is one of the well known water colours by the son of the Baptist Minster of Fleet, William Burgess, done during the residence of Maurice Johnson DD and dated 1818, signed HB (Hilkiah Burgess). All the front windows have been changed again, and spikes have appeared on the wooden porch. He portrays two matching gothic windows in the tower which are shown in the painted panel. There are three turrets on the tower; this seems to vary from two to four, perhaps one is the garderobe turret.

The Back - this is a much copied Burgess, dated 1818. The bay is shown but all the windows seem quite oddly irregular, some with lintels and one looking Venetian. The north extension has been built with a large chimney over the new kitchen range. Someone is cutting the creeper hiding the back door, and there are new gates in the wall. The kitchen is operating with its tall chimney smoking. The tower is clearly painted with its windows. There is a pump by the door, which leads into the south cross wing. Next to the bay window is a chimney-like structure, not shown on the Nattes, but the 'frilly' window has survived. The chimney-like structure is of equal height with the bay window and it appears it have two loop-like windows. It is still there now.

The South West Side - Another Burgess, undated unfortunately, but showing the south-western aspect from the river.. From this angle the turret is shown, but he has painted eleven windows along the southern façade. There is a high wall along the side of the garden with a wooden barrier near the river with small barges or fishing boats moored. The impact of the bay windows on the front is emphasised along with the Dutch gabling.

With the arrival of the 6th Maurice Johnson in 1834, 'the Major', many changes took place during his short time there (he left in 1851 to live finally in Blundeston, Suffolk), Ayscoughfee suffered a transformation and was disguised as Tudoresque. During the 1840s the whole front was changed for ever. The two gables were partially rebuilt with strangely shaped in the Dutch style. Two large crenellated stone bay windows were erected on to the front. A long screen or covered porch with stone pillars replaced the small porch. New Elizabethan type chimneys and cloisters were installed and a huge coat of arms appears. The wooden windows were replaced with rectangular stone. The tower was made rectangular and extended upwards. In 1845 a 6ft. heraldic device topped with Valkyrie wings (it is intended to be an raven) was placed aloft. (In an earthquake in 1930 it fell down and smashed, but was unfortunately replaced almost immediately). The triangular pediment with a window was removed. New kitchens were installed in the north extension (see Rushbury painting).

The South Lawn - In this postcard, dating from 1920, the garden room is clearly shown with two large French windows. All of the windows on this side, including one bricked-up and covered with ivy, are 18th/19th century.

The suggestion is that this 'garden room' was built by one of the long-term tenants - probably Mr. Bonner (1874-96), but an extension of some sort on this side of the house is also shown on a 1779 map by Armstrong.

Rear aspect - An original oil painting by Henry Rushbury RA painted c.1936 shows a very complicated building of the north wing, and the extension is shown with Gayton close to it. The bay window is squeezed but a bell is shown on the top, and the false column is much taller. Tall bushes and trees hide the back up to window height, a tall door is shown in the kitchen wing and windows have three casements and a lintel. What might be a courtyard is shown with turrets, and the gable has been shaped in imitation of the front. There are more chimney stacks than at present, but the greatest change since the Burgess views is the larger kitchen wing to the north.

1912 – This postcard clearly shows the iron railings at the front of the Hall. The roof of Holyrood House is just visible to the left. Note the two boats on the (rather high) river, which are similar in style to those on the Burgess miniature.

1941 – This view of the tennis courts (laid out in 1925) also gives a clear view of the rear of the Hall (including the bell cote above the bay window) and a good view if its neighbour, Holyrood House.

The Great Hall

The great hall in Ayscoughfee would have looked something like this until the ceiling was installed at around the end of the 18th century.

The picture on the left is, in fact, the Great Hall at Gainsborough Old Hall in north Lincolnshire, built by Sir Thomas Burgh around 1460. The contemporary construction dates of the two buildings makes comparisons of their various original features inevitable.

Ayscoughfee would have had a central hearth, with the smoke rising to escape through a louvre in the roof, like the one here at Gainsborough

The louvre at Ayscoughfee was probably removed when the hall was divided during the time of the Evingtons.

Unfortunately, the garderobe turrets have not been preserved, but one in the tower at the Old Hall, gives a good idea of what one would have looked like.

Originally they would have had wooden doors, and would have also been used to store clothing, as the smell would help to repel moths, lice and fleas!

The contents of the garderobes would be collected and mixed with the ashes from the fireplaces, and provided an invaluable source of fertiliser.

Plans of The Gardens

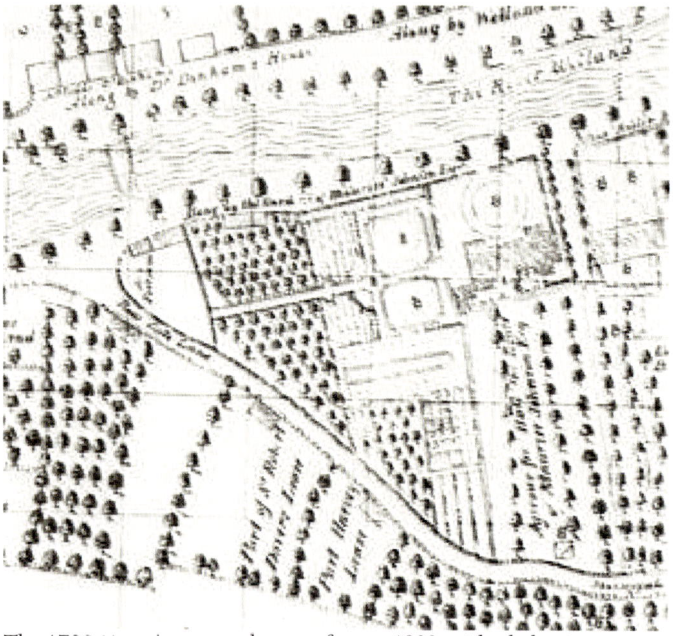

The 1732 Grundy map and a page from a 1903 guide (below), with acknowledgement to Spalding Gentlemen's Society

1903 Ordnance Survey map
with acknowledgement to Alan Godfrey Maps Ltd

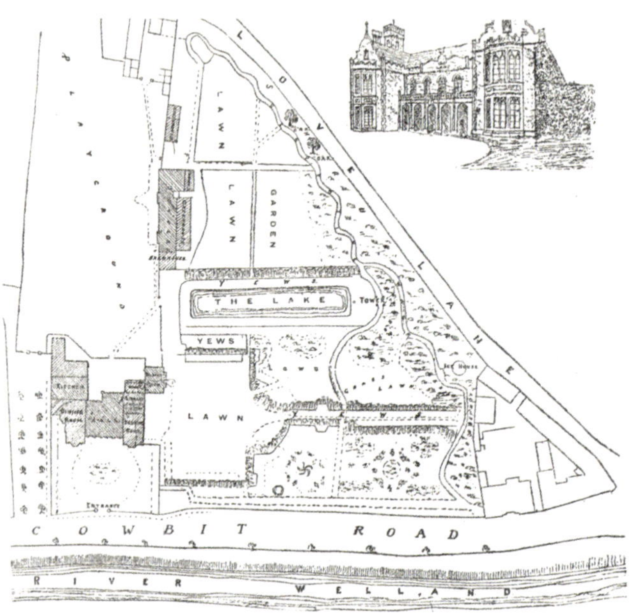

Possible site of one of the gatehouses on Newgate (now Love Lane) leading to the service wing ?

The Ice House

The first recorded ice house in Britain was built at Greenwich in 1619.

The popularity of these structures peaked in the eighteenth century, when no aristocratic estate was without one.

Further research is required to determine the exact age of the ice house in the gardens, but it is not shown on the 1732 Grundy map. Although it might be the feature shown on the Armstrong map of 1779.

Doorway into the ice house

The Memorial Fountain

The fountain standing in the gardens was originally installed in Hall Place in 1874 at a cost of £300, as a memorial to Miss Mary Johnson, who had given £1500 towards providing a mains water supply for the town. With her sister Miss Elizabeth Johnson (both of Fairfax House, [later Holyrood]) the ladies were among the principal contributors towards the building of the Johnson Hospital in 1881. Mary Johnson also contributed to the building of St Peter's Church (1876-1968) which stood opposite the hospital in Priory Road on the site of the Council offices.

The Turret

Let us now briefly turn to the turret, the irregular pentagon which houses the main staircase to the Ailwyn's private quarters.

Left – The current appearance. Some of the damaged, delicate pierced stonework was replaced during the refurbishment.

The (undated) Hilkiah Burgess print shows it in this current form, along with the stone bay windows of the cross-wings which were remodelled in the 1840s.

The 1818 Burgess rear view

The 1818 Burgess front view. The roof appears to be pentagonal, and possibly lead covered.

The Brand engraving of 1808(left), and the Everard watercolour (undated), both show an ornate flagpole and pennant.

The 1791 Nattes looks similar to the 1818 picture.

Finally, the oak panel. This looks substantially identical to the 1818 view.

CHAPTER 15

CONUNDRUM

For several centuries the only buildings along Church Gate were a group of houses on the corner near High Bridge. Later, Bergery House (now the Old White Horse Inn), said to be built from the Priory remains (and the home of the Willesby family, next door to the old rope walk – now a Cantonese restaurant) led into fields and gardens. All along Church Gate, opposite the river, were trees, orchards and gardens, until the two grand houses were reached. Gayton and Ayscoughfee, with a wide, tree-lined path between them and their large gardens spreading out to the entrance of Newgate (now Love Lane), so called because it was newly developed. Here were two high status houses, lived in by prosperous people, surrounded by estates with outhouses and stables, two highly desirable residences.

Between 1709 and 1898 both houses were in the same ownership. The Johnson family owned both and all the occupants can be identified. During this time there must have been interchange when the same family owned both.

As no-one knows when these plots were first built on, or who owned them originally, guesswork must play a part in all of this. The key name, Ayscoughfee, suggests an ancient origin. It is old English for the place of the ash trees. Ash trees still grow vigorous and unwanted in this area. But it must all be conjecture.

When Gooch mentions 'Reginald and Isabella Gayton generosus' at Gayton House in 1480, he alone mentions them but they appear to be well ensconced and are perhaps middle-aged.[1] The house called after them for so long makes their presence there a reasonable certainty. Gooch does not suggest they built the house, and they may have lived there for some time, but only he knew their name, and the inference is he saw some document, no longer available to us, to find their exact names and the word generosus. I can find no other reference to their presence in Spalding, except by Maddison, writing much later.

What cannot yet be finally established is whether the original Gaytons stayed at Gayton until the arrival of the Hobsons in about 1600, and whether the Halls were in residence next door as it appears they were during this time. It is, of course, possible that the Gaytons were established long before 1480 and owned the whole plot, selling off the part that is now Ayscoughfee.[2]

It is possible the Gaytons were there first, as their house has every appearance of being much the oldest, with its outside staircase, smaller rooms and timber framing, stables as part of the house, a much older design. As mentioned earlier, this building seems to have originally been a medieval Guildhall.

By 1600, the Hobson family are well documented, 1600-1684, living at Gayton House. The Gayton family disappeared from the records. Reginald and Isabella Gayton may have had just the one daughter, who married William Hall, the family of Halls inherited it through her, and it passed through them. The Hobsons may have been tenants only (one Hobson girl married a Hall in 1620) but in 1684 William Ambler bought Gayton House and the rest is history. Maurice Johnson the Antiquary married Elizabeth Ambler, William's heiress, and so inherited Gayton House. The Johnsons' ownership of Gayton House lasted until 1898 when Alderman FitzAlan Howard of Long Sutton acquired it, until it was sold to a cinema company and eventually demolished by the local council in 1959. It was this heinous action that spawned the Spalding & District Civic Society.

Long before the houses were in joint occupation by the Johnson family, the Gayton family reappeared. Exactly when is not altogether clear, but by some strange coincidence there were two lots of people with the same names, one Reginald and Robert Gayton, and one Reginald and Robert Hall, one pair were brothers, the others father and son.

---

1. Generosus cannot be translated accurately, but it connotes prosperous people, of good family.
2. Two manors are mentioned for this area, one is the Royal Manor belonging to the King or Queen personally, and the other Spalding-cum-Membris.

Their son, or grandson, Simon Hall of Burton Pedwardine, married Juliana Roberts for his first wife. She died in 1556. She was born a Roberts of Donington (her father) and (it seems) her mother-in-law, William Hall's wife, an unnamed Gayton, whose mother was Isabella. Upon Juliana's death, her son Reginald Hall inherited Ayscoughfee from her. From the burial place of Reginald's wife Mary (died 1565) and their only child Jane (died in the same year) it appears they settled in Spalding. Reginald's children Anne, Jane, Elizabeth all died. They were based in Spalding between 1579 and 1582. If they continued to live at Gayton House this would fill the 100 years between 1480 and 1602. Could the Halls have lived at Ayscoughfee while the Gaytons lived next door?

Finally, the conundrum; I think there is a glimpse of a long drawn out family feud between the Gaytons and the Halls, as there seems little doubt that both houses were in the occupation of the Halls at one time or another, and it may be both were in the occupation of the Gaytons. How did Juliana Roberts, marrying a Hall, acquire Ayscoughfee? There is no doubt the Halls owned Ayscoughfee because Robert sold it in 1602. She could not have inherited it from her mother, a Roberts. It might have been *his* mother, a Gayton, who left Ayscoughfee to Juliana, who in turn left it to her son, Reginald, whose son Robert sold Ayscoughfee to Wimberley. He died in 1627. Perhaps she bought it for some reason.

For Juliana to leave Ayscoughfee freely to her son (she was not a widow) it could not have been acquired by marriage. She was limited to bequeathing her property by certain restrictions. To complicate things further there is the peculiar situation that Simon Hall was the common grandfather of both Robert and Reginald. This does seem quite incredible but it seems there arose a dispute between the two lots of Reginald and Robert as to their inheritances, which rumbled on at least until 1602, the two Gayton brothers (Reginald and Robert) contesting the inheritance of the two Halls, father and son (Reginald and Robert), even though the two Gaytons were dead.

It is apodictic that the Halls owned Ayscoughfee because Robert sold it in 1602 to the Wimberleys. But how did they obtain it? The many famous Spalding families, the Oldfields, Wimberleys, Gamlyns, Amblers, Evingtons, Gaytons, Halls, Johnsons, Ogles and Ailwyns were all related by marriage, but to work out all the exact descents, particularly when they go back to before the 15th century, is well nigh impossible.

The common grandfather, Simon Hall, who died in 1565, was grandfather to Robert and Reginald Hall and to Robert and Reginald Gayton. There must be a missing link somewhere, such as a Hall daughter marrying a Gayton son. The Gaytons' grievance (if it was such) must have been that the Halls finished up with Ayscoughfee.

The Gaytons were soon complaining that their land had been taken from them. There is only a snippet about it but it is a tantalizing one:

'Robert Gayton petitions to King and Council regarding his lands in Lincolnshire, Spalding, Pinchbeck, Gosberton and Stamford. Endorsed by Reginald Gayton of London.' [1]

It appears that a Robert Gayton had properties in London near St. Mary le Bow in about 1441[2] together with a Walter Gayton. There is no proof that this Gayton is any relation to the Robert Gayton who was dead by 1602, except the coincidence of the names.

The dispute also involves the Ailwyns. In his will Nicholas speaks as if Robert Gayton was his uncle, half brother or brother and the first conclusion to jump at is that Margaret, his mother was either a Gayton before marriage or by another marriage to a Gayton. She could have been a Gayton by birth. No mention is ever made of Nicholas' wife's name, age or date of death or place of burial. Nothing is known of her. Mistress Gayton, first of the mourners, is mentioned in Nicholas' will. Could this be his mother-in-law?

---

1. *National Archives Special Collection* (Ancient Petitions) XI SC8. Unfortunately, undated but 15th century. No follow-up has been found.
2. *Historical Gazeteer of London before the Great Fire, Cheapside*. Keen & Harding 1987.

The Hall family feature in Maddison and were armigerous;[1] there were numerous branches Hall of Donnington, Hall[2] of Grantham, Hall of Snarford and Hall of Spalding. William Hall of County Nottingham married a daughter of Reginald Gayton of Spalding. Unfortunately, her name is not recorded. The Gaytons were fond of the names Reginald and Robert. The Gaytons were related in some way to the Ailwyn family.

Nicholas Ailwyn said[3] in his long will:
"After my decease kepe an obite or anniversary in the Parish Church of Spalding for my soule, the soules of my fader and moder and of our children and of R. Garton (Gayton?) and for all Christian soules." And later: *"Souls of Ric. Alwyn and Margaret his wife of me Nicholas Alwyn their son Robert Gayton and all Christian souls."*

I have not seen the original. In the absence of any punctuation, Robert Gayton could be another son. 'Squire Gayton' could be R. Gayton - all the same person.

Another glimpse of the Gayton family's claim appears in the 1602 conveyance, when Robert Hall sold Ayscoughfee to Thomas Wimberley.[4] (shown below)

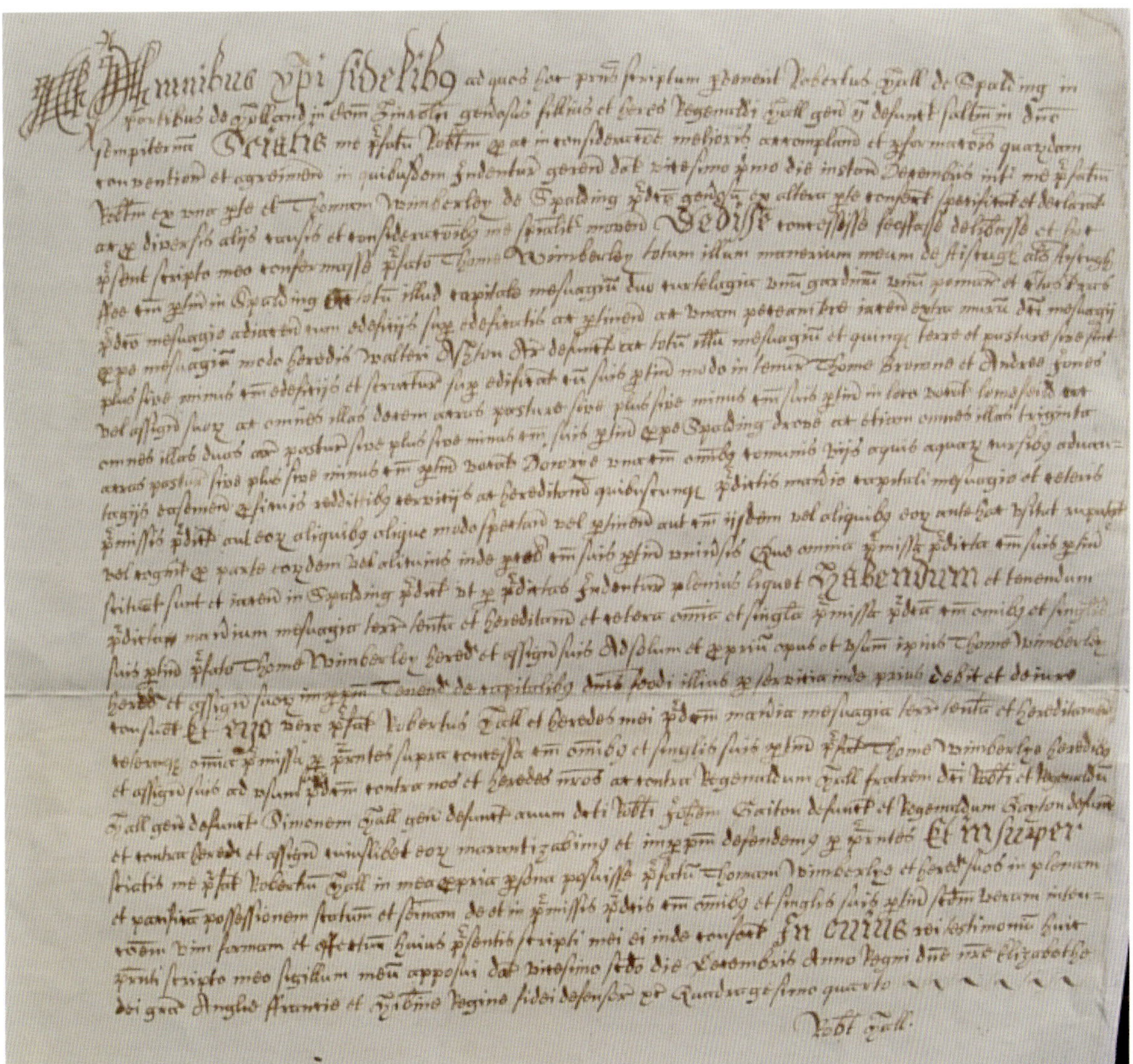

1. Argent a chevron engrailed between 3 talbots heads erased sable within a border gules. This coat appears in the glass window in Ayscoughfee.
2. Only Hall of Grantham was related to Spalding Halls.
3. Will of Nicholas Ailwyn, Alderman of London. (Pro prob 11/75 1505-6) Not admitted to probate until 1518. It is not yet known whether this will was contested, or what caused the delay.
4. Dated 26th December 1602, the conveyance gives a warranty (against claims) by Robert Hall (the vendor) and his brother Reginald, and of Reginald his father, and Simon Hall deceased (grandfather of the said Robert John Gaiton deceased and Reginald Gayton deceased) and claims by their heirs and assigns.

This demonstrates that the Gaytons had some claim or interest in Ayscoughfee, which was still alive and a threat, although both Simon Hall[1] and the two Gaytons were all dead. There may be other explanations or interpretations and much more enquiry is needed, but there is little doubt that the Gaytons continued to contest Ayscoughfee or threatened to do so through their heirs.[2]

It all happened so long ago. The time spent searching out the details of such an ancient dispute may not be fruitful academically and a solution may never be found, but the long dead participants have lived again for this enquiry.

Copy of the 1658 conveyance of Ayscoughfee between Sir John Walpole and John Johnson of Pinchbeck. The house is sold for £400.

1. See Hall of Spalding. P444 of Maddison (*Lincolnshire Families*)
2. Robert Hall's sale of Ayscoughfee (1602) 26th December 1602. All the land tenants are named in the deed but the house itself is not let out.

APPENDIX A: BERINGITA

There still remains the unexplored question of the one and only reference to "*Feod de Askehughe*" in the Valor Ecclesiasticus of 1535. Is this any evidence of the Ascoughs' presence in Spalding, or of their connection with house?

Spalding, being ancient, was divided into several manors which are roughly known.[1] There is Spalding Manor, Syon, Spalding-cum-Membris, Monkshall, Town End (Ducks Hall) and Spalding-cum-Crowland, formerly known as Berewita or Beringita.[2]

The dates and facts of the foundation of Spalding Priory are a contentious topic, but this is one version. In the time of the Danish invasions, Crowland Abbey had been burnt and pillaged by the Danes and there was a famine. Thorald de Bokenhale, acting for his father, the Duke of Mercia, attended by Wulfgeat, Abbot of Crowland, founded in Spalding for six of the displaced Crowland monks, a cell on Easter Day 1051. He endowed it with a Manor, called Berewita. This is the only Crowland property in Spalding.[3]

Grundy marks it on his 1732 map of Spalding. It was along Double Street and is marked clearly as Berewita, Spalding, Crowland on the west side of the Welland. There is no suggestion of any extension to the east.

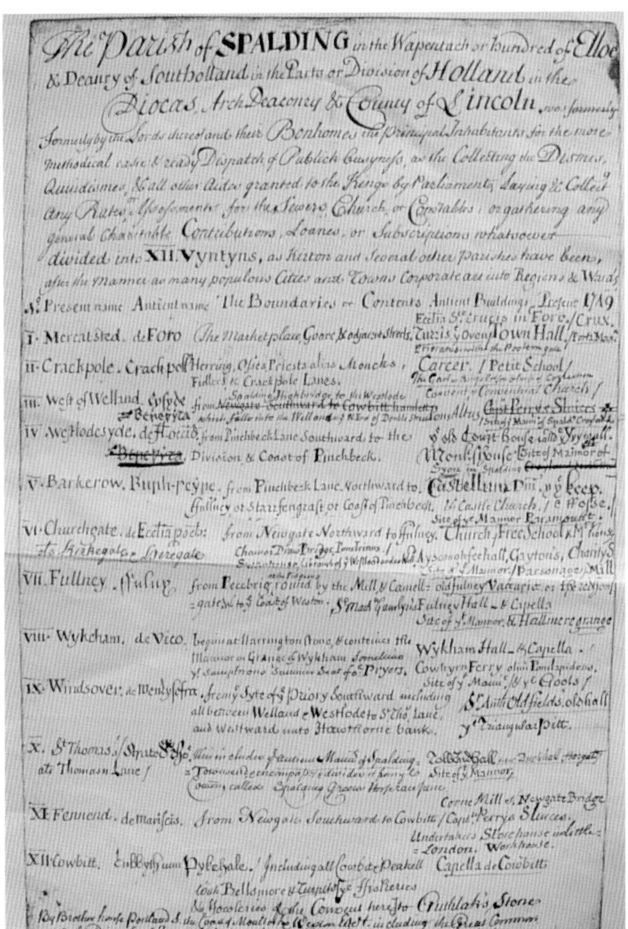
The Parish of SPALDING in the Wapentach or Hundred of Elloe & Deanry of Southolland in the Parts or Division of Holland in the Dioces, Arch Deaconry & County of Lincoln
...
divided into XII. Vyntyns
...

Copy of Johnson's 1749 document

Maurice Johnson's project to divide Spalding into small portions relied on manors as boundaries. There seems to have been some doubt in his mind. He writes:

"*IV. Westlodesyde de fl occid from Pinchbeck Lane southward to the division coast of Pinchbeck. Monks house site of manor of Syon in Spalding and the old town house called Ivy Wall. Berewita.*"

"*III. West of Welland from Newgate southward to Cowbit hamlet. Captain Perry's sluice gate site of manor of Spalding-Crowland.*"

He corrected this by crossing Berewita off (IV) and inserting it in III, crossing off Newgate Southward to Cowbit hamlet and inserting Spalding High bridge to the Westlode and crossing off Captain Perry's sluices.

So his Vyntyn III is 'west of the Welland, from the highbridge to the Westlode at the north end of Double Street, the site of the Manor of Spalding-Crowland'. No mention of any land on the east of the Welland. So the "*Feod de Askehughe*" is not the site of Ayscoughfee, and the reference is not as important as it seems.

1. In an evaluation of church lands ordered by Henry VIII, Crowland Abbey is recorded as paying a small rent for lands in Spalding, which does not prove anything.
2. Beringita's areas was 2 carucates, about 40 acres, and is marked on the Grundy map (as Beremith) along Double Street.
3. He gave the site of the manor to 'God and St. Guthlac in Frankalmoyn', a feudal tenure involving no services except praying for the soul of the donor.

APPENDIX B: SCANDINAVIAN ORIGINS

Drawing a long shot, in the complete absence of reliable clues, it seems possible that the whole site on the west brink was a very early one, and that the name Ayscoughfee could have its origin in much earlier times. There is a word, Aiskew or Echescol, which could refer to ash or oak trees. In Scandinavian, Etkiskogr is oakwood. Eski is old Norse for a places with ash trees. Akeshengh – Ake meaning oak, hengh being wood. Or Akeshaw – shaw meaning wood. Ascow is ashwood, a Scandinavian compound from Askr with Skogr.[1]

This would appear to refer to an ash or oakwood, or the place where they grew trees, common in this area, so it is quite possible that dim memories of this language survived in folk memory, and the Ayscough family of north Lincolnshire had no connections.[2] The fen folk of Lincolnshire have long memories and many early words are still to be seen in field and street names in the county, and in what remains of the dialect.[3] Scandinavian languages still were spoken in parts of Lincolnshire in the 19th century.

Late 1950s Postcard, showing the roof of the stable block and ancient yews before they were destroyed by fire in the early 70s

1. See *Anglo Saxon Dictionary*, Clark-Hall.
2. Tradition has it that there was an earlier house on the site (Maurice Johnson)
3. *A History of English Place Names*. John Field. P.62

APPENDIX C: THE JOHNSON HEIRS

Martin Johnson of Sutterton Attorney	~m~	*Wife unknown*
	4 sons survived	
Martin Johnson (1588-1650)	~m (1) ~ ~m (2) ~ ~m (3) ~	(1) Eleanor Burton (d.1609) (2) Elizabeth *unknown* (d.1617) (3) Jane Lynne (d. 1655)
	12 children ~ only 5 survived	
Walter Johnson (1619-c.1680)	~m (1)16?? ~ ~m (2)1657 ~	(1) Agnes Willesby (d.16??) (2) Katherine King (d.1697) née Downs
10 children ~ only 3 survived (Maurice [1], and Martin & Mary - who left Spalding)		
Maurice Johnson [1] (1661-1747) Barrister	~m (1)1683 ~ ~m (2)1705 ~ ~m (3)1726 ~	(1) Jane Johnson (1666-1703) (2) Elizabeth Oldfield (d.1724) (3) Anne Wood (d.1741)
	8 children ~ only Maurice [2] survived	
Maurice Johnson [2] (1688-1755) Barrister "The Antiquary"	~m 1709 ~	Elizabeth Ambler (1690-1754) (Grand-daughter of Sir Anthony Oldfield)
	26 children ~ only 12 survived	
Col. **Maurice Johnson** [3] (1714-1793) Duke of Cumberland's Regiment	~m (1)17?? ~ ~m (2)17?? ~	(1) Elizabeth Bellamy (d.1752) (2) Mary Baker (d.1773)
	2 sons & 3 daughters	
Dr. **Maurice Johnson** DD [4] (1756-1834) Vicar of Moulton & Spalding	~m 1779 ~	Anne Buckworth (1752-1827)
	3 sons & 1 daughter	
Rev. **Maurice Johnson** MA [5] (1788-1820) Curate at Moulton	~m 1814 ~	Frances Post (1786-1815) died after childbirth
One son, Maurice [6] who was raised by grand-parents at Ayscoughfee		
Major **Maurice Johnson** BA [6] (1815-1864) Royal South Lincoln Militia	~m (1)1841 ~ ~m (2)1848 ~	(1) Elizabeth Mills (d.1843) (2) Isabella Swan (d.1905)
	5 daughters - 4 survived	

SUBSCRIBERS

(IN ALPHABETICAL ORDER)

I would like to thank the following for their generosity (and patience) in the production of this book.

Katie Ball, Langdon Hills, Essex
Jonathan Biggadike, Spalding, Lincs.
Leslie Bourne, Spalding, Lincs.
Sheena & Paul Brockett, Spalding, Lincs.
Andrew & Mary Burnet, Spalding, Lincs.
Michael Byrd, Spalding, Lincs.
Rodney & Janet Callow, Lincoln
Barbara Clark, Spalding, Lincs.
Mrs Rose Clarke, Spalding, Lincs.
C L Evans, Thorney, Cambs
Edward Hall, Spalding, Lincs.
Mr & Mrs Hall, Spalding, Lincs.
Mrs M Hand, Spalding, Lincs.
John Haresign, Spalding, Lincs.
Mr & Mrs D Harpham, Spalding, Lincs.
John Honnor, Holbeach, Lincs.
Revd & Mrs Hulme, Spalding, Lincs.
Andrew Inkley, Spalding, Lincs.
Mr & Mrs David Jones, Long Sutton, Lincs.
Mr & Mrs David Jones, Spalding, Lincs.
Paul McCarthy, Spalding, Lincs.
Andy Metcalfe, West Pinchbeck, Lincs.
Alan Moore, Spalding, Lincs.
Hilary Nethersole, Reading, Berks
Angela Newton, Spalding, Lincs.
James Nicholson, Stanwick, Northants
Stuart Parkin, Spalding, Lincs.
Andrew Parsons, Spalding, Lincs.
Graham Paulin, Spalding, Lincs.
Mr & Mrs A Pearce, Moulton Chapel, Lincs.
John Pett, Spalding, Lincs.
Mrs I Pollard, Spalding, Lincs.
Ian Pollard & Clare McBride, Spalding, Lincs.
Mr & Mrs Rawlins, Spalding, Lincs.
Paul Redford, Spalding, Lincs.
Sheila Robson MBE, Spalding, Lincs.
Ben Runciman, Weston, Lincs.
Dr Richard & Mrs Rachel Smith, Little Staughton, Beds
Clare Robertson, Pinchbeck, Lincs.
John Tinsley, Spalding, Lincs.
Tom Taylor, Spilsby, Lincs.
Patrick Wensor, Spalding, Lincs.
Mr & Mrs A Wensor, Spalding, Lincs.
Mr & Mrs J Wensor, Spalding, Lincs.
Mavis Wilson, Spalding, Lincs.
Nick Worth, Holbeach St Marks, Lincs.

INDEX

View from the Tower – Autumn 2005